BARRON'S
BUSINESS KEYS

KEYS TO INCORPORATING

Third Edition

Steven A. Fox, LL.M., C.P.A.

Attorney-at-Law
Palm Beach, Florida

SO-BZX-786

BARRON'S

All inquiries should be addressed to:
Barron's Educational Series, Inc.
250 Wireless Boulevard
Hauppauge, NY 11788
http://www.barronseduc.com

Library of Congress Catalog Card Number 00-042911

International Standard Book Number 0-7641-1300-3

**Library of Congress Cataloging-in-Publication
Data**
Fox, Steven A.
  Keys to incorporating / Steven A. Fox — 3rd ed.
    p. cm. — (Barron's business keys)
  Includes index.
  ISBN 0-7641-1300-3 (alk. paper)
  1. Incorporation — United States. 2. Corporate Law —
United States. 3. Corporations — Taxations — Law and
legislation — United States. I. Title. II. Series.
  KF1420.F69   2001
  346.73'06622—dc21
                                    00-042911
                                      CIP

PRINTED IN THE UNITED STATES OF AMERICA
9 8 7 6 5 4 3 2 1

CONTENTS

1

INTRODUCTION TO BUSINESS ORGANIZATION

Selecting the form of doing business is one of the first decisions the owner of an enterprise must make. Should the business be a proprietorship, a partnership, or a corporation? Even after the choice has been made, circumstances may trigger a change in the nature of the business, so that the best form at one time may not be the best at another.

The basis for making a sensible choice of business form rests on commercial law and tax regulations, which are different in their effects on the various forms of doing business. An initial consideration is whether the enterprise is to be a not-for-profit concern or a for-profit concern. This book concentrates on the latter category.

Broadly speaking, the forms of for-profit enterprise in the United States can be divided into two areas, noncorporate and corporate. Principal noncorporate forms include the sole proprietorship, the general partnership, and the limited partnership. The corporate forms may be divided into regular (C) corporations and S corporations. The distinction between regular (C) and S corporations is an important one, relating to two subchapters of the federal tax law applying different tax treatment to closely held businesses from that for other corporate enterprises. Other classifications of for-profit entities exist as well, such as the land trust and the Massachusetts business trust. However, for purposes of space, only the major types will be considered in this book.

The *sole proprietorship* is the noncorporate form for a business having only one owner. It represents the simplest and most inexpensive form to organize, operate, and terminate, but it is inconvenient to transfer to another owner. Further, the amount of investment capital one can raise is limited. As distinct from partnerships or corporations, which can look to other sources for funds, sole proprietors must provide the total investment for their businesses either themselves or through borrowing. Since the sole proprietorship and its owner are identical for tax and nontax purposes, the proprietor has *unlimited liability* for the obligations of the business. Although federal tax law requires the sole proprietor to maintain separate books and records for the business, all federal income tax consequences of the business flow directly to the proprietor.

The general partnership and limited partnership forms are the noncorporate forms for businesses having more than one owner. The Uniform Partnership Act (UPA) provides that a partnership is an association of two or more persons to carry on as co-owners for profit. Partnerships are basically of two types—commercial partnerships and personal service partnerships. In the latter, there is rarely any substantial inventory or fixed assets, since the income of the enterprise is derived from the services rendered by the partners.

A general partnership lacks continuity of life, centralization of management, and free transferability of interests, although the partnership agreement may allow for some of these characteristics. In the general partnership, the general partners have unlimited liability for the debts and obligations of the partners. Further, the partners are jointly and severally liable for torts and breaches of trust injuring third parties, meaning that the action may be brought against any single partner without joining the others. However, the partners are jointly but not severally liable on all partnership debts and contracts, so that a contract creditor may not proceed against a single creditor. In such case, under what is known as compulsory joinder, the partner sued can generally force the joinder of all of the remaining partners, who are deemed to be necessary parties to the action. In a limited partnership, a specified group of partners—called the limited partners—may invest their money and share in the returns while limiting their liability to the amount of their contributions. In any partnership there must be at least one general partner. It is important to note that the limited partners, unlike general partners, lack decisional authority. In fact, if limited partners exercise any control over the business, they lose their special limited liability status. From an organizational standpoint, the principal difference between the general and the limited partnership is that a general partnership is a means for carrying on an operating business, whereas the limited partnership is largely an investment vehicle.

A partnership is not a taxable entity but must determine its profit or loss and file an "information return" on Form 1065. Since no tax is paid by the partnership, the partners are taxed as individuals on their *distributive* shares of partnership taxable income, whether they have received the cash or not, and even if the partnership agreement requires that the money actually be retained in the business as partnership capital.

Note: A joint venture is a type of temporary partnership organized to carry on a business venture for profit. This is distinct from the partnership or corporation organized to carry on a business for an indefinite period. Although not discussed here, there are also special rules for publicly traded partnerships which are treated as corporations rather than as partnerships, although the traditional tests would qualify them as the latter. Simply stated, a publicly traded partnership is one whose interests are traded on an established securities market or are readily tradable on a secondary market or the substantial equivalent of such a market. A master limited partnership is a publicly traded partnership consisting of a parent limited partnership and one or more subsidiary partnerships

3

that own the assets of the business. Generally, income from publicly traded partnerships is treated as portfolio income for purposes of the passive loss rules, meaning that income from a publicly traded partnership cannot be offset with losses from passive activities.

A business in a corporate form is generally treated as a separate entity for both tax and nontax purposes. The income of a regular (C) corporation may be taxed first to the corporation, then to the shareholders as dividends, and, with the passage of the Tax Reform Act of 1986, again at both the corporate and shareholder levels on liquidation. This should be contrasted with the S corporation, which has most of the characteristics of a regular (C) corporation but which is generally not treated as a separate taxable entity. Thus, the S corporation is a pass-through entity somewhat akin to the partnership, with items of income, deduction, loss, and credit said to flow through directly to the shareholders.

This concept will be considered in greater detail later. For the present, it should be noted that much lower tax rates apply to the first $75,000 of corporate taxable income for the regular (C) corporation. The 34 percent corporate tax rate takes effect at $75,000 of taxable income, although personal service corporations pay tax on all their earnings at a flat 35 percent rate. The problem with C corporations is that when the corporate earnings are distributed in the form of dividends, a second tier of tax is imposed on the earnings at individual tax rates up to 39.6 percent. Notwithstanding this two-tier tax, C corporations offer a good deal of flexibility, since there are no rules on such points as who may own the stock or how many classes of stock may be outstanding. In an S corporation, which has such limitations, there may be no more than 75 shareholders, no more than a single class of stock, and so forth. The main advantage of an S corporation is that the earnings pass through from the corporation directly to the shareholders, who pay tax on that income at their individual tax rates, again at a maximum effective rate of

39.6 percent. Since the tax rates on S corporation share-holders are lower than those for C corporations until their corporate taxable income reaches $335,000, many taxpayers choose to operate as S corporations (under Subchapter S of the Internal Revenue Code) before opting for regular corporate tax status (under Subchapter C of the Internal Revenue Code).

At the state level, some states conform their tax treatment to the federal code but some do not. Thus, New Jersey and New York tax S corporations on the difference between the taxes they would pay as regular (C) corporations and as individual taxpayers.

The corporate form is chosen by many entrepreneurs because of its core attributes—limited liability, continuity of life, centralization of management, and free transferability of interests. *Limited liability* means that the shareholders generally risk no more than their total investment in the business. This can be extremely important. If there is an unanticipated reversal in business conditions that causes a corporation to start losing money and, perhaps eventually, to default on its loans, the shareholders are not held personally liable to make good on those losses and loans.

Continuity of life refers to the fact that corporations are generally established with perpetual existence. Thus, the death, disability, or withdrawal of a shareholder—even the controlling shareholder—will not necessarily terminate corporate existence. A corporation offers *centralization of management* in that the board of directors has exclusive authority to make management and business decisions on behalf of the corporation. (A limited partnership generally possesses this attribute, too, in that the general partners have continuing exclusive authority to make management and business decisions). Corporate shares of stock are often more *freely transferred* than are partnership interests. However, in corporations owned and managed by a relatively small number of persons (known as closely held corporations), shares may not be disposed of easily if there is no ready market for the securities and if the shares are subject to restrictions on transferability.

This book will focus on the role of the closely held corporation, which is becoming a form of choice for the small businessperson. In particular, the advantages and disadvantages of the S corporation will be described and evaluated. This book will also consider a special form of closely held corporation, the professional service corporation. State laws authorize the formation of corporations to render professional services such as medicine, dentistry, and accounting, which are now subject to a flat federal corporate tax rate of 35 percent. All the shareholders (and generally all the directors and officers) must be licensed to practice the particular profession in the state.

A newer form, the limited liability company, will also be considered in Key 9. Essentially, the limited liability company blends the corporate characteristic of limited liability with the beneficial pass-through single-taxation tax treatment afforded partnerships and S corporations.

Incorporation is governed by individual state laws, among which there is considerable variation. Fortunately, most states follow either the Model Business Corporation Act (MBCA) or, more recently, the revised version (RMBCA). Thus, most of the explanations in the Keys that follow will be based on these models. Corporate formalities as prescribed by law must be observed in even the smallest corporations. It is important for entrepreneurs and owners to understand that the corporation is a separate entity, subject not only to governmental laws and regulations but also to its own articles of incorporation and bylaws. A corporation may enter into contracts in its own name, hold, convey, and receive property, and sue and be sued. In the federal courts, a corporation is deemed to be a citizen in the state in which it has its principal place of business as well as in the state in which it is incorporated.

2

THE INCORPORATION PROCESS

This Key is intended to present an overview of the incorporation process and some related federal and state laws. The emphasis will be on the attorney-client relationship.

Businesspeople interested in incorporation should meet with an attorney in a preincorporation conference. Provisions of the articles of incorporation ("articles") and other instruments required by law are discussed to ensure that their content is fully understood by all concerned. If there is more than one principal involved, is the attorney representing the majority interest, the minority interest, or both? There is a potential conflict of interest here.

An initial consideration is the proposed name for the corporation. This is an important step. It is worth noting that filing the approved name in the articles with the secretary of state's office does not imply that the use of a name will not violate some other law (see Key 4).

The next consideration is whether a preincorporation agreement or subscription agreement should be adopted by the parties. A preincorporation agreement is simply a contract to create a corporation, whereas a subscription agreement is a contract for the purchase of corporate stock. These two agreements may be combined into one. There is a great deal of ground to be covered in a preincorporation agreement. First, the contracting parties should state that the corporation will be formed under and pursuant to state law. They should then indicate what the name, purposes, duration, and registered office and agent of the corporation will be, the fact that the corporation will be under the management of a board of directors ("board"), what capital contributions/loans will be made, how much the authorized capital stock will be, and who shall be the incorporator(s). The function of the incorporator(s) is a mere formality; in fact, an incorporator has no authority and no duties other than to sign the corporate articles. Other points that should be covered in the preincorporation agreement are whether cumulative voting and preemptive rights will be permitted; whether the corporation agrees to indemnify directors and/or officers against errors and omissions committed by them; who the initial shareholders will be and their respective share ownership; Section 1244 implications; whether the board or shareholders can act without a meeting; what expenses incurred qualify for reimbursement; whether there will be a covenant not to compete (even where permitted by state law such covenants must be reasonable as to time and area); what will happen in the event of corporate deadlock; where the principal offices of the business will be located; and how the preincorporation agreement may be terminated.

In a subscription agreement, the prospective shareholders—known as the subscribers—each promise to purchase a specified amount of stock from the corporation for a specified price. (In some states, an incorporator must subscribe to at least one share.) Such an agreement may be executed before or after the corporation is formed and is generally irrevocable for six months, except by consent of all subscribers or as otherwise provided in the agreement. It is good practice, nevertheless, to specify the term of the subscription in the agreement. If the amount due under a subscription agreement is not paid when due, the corporation may collect the amount in the same manner as any debt due from a third-party debtor. Moreover, the agreement may provide for other penalties.

The next consideration is preparation of the articles

of incorporation and bylaws. For the articles there are two types of provisions—mandatory and permissive. Mandatory provisions include, for example, the corporate name (which must contain a word like *corporation* to indicate that the enterprise is a corporation); the corporate purpose (e.g., to engage in any activities or business permitted under state law); the registered office and agent; the names and addresses of the initial board of directors; the names and addresses of the incorporators; and the authorized capital, which generally refers to the aggregate number, par value, and class or classes of shares the corporation is authorized to issue. Although par value historically represented the expected selling price of the shares, today shares may be issued with or without a stated par value. Nevertheless, stock having a par value may not be issued for consideration worth less than the aggregate par value of the issued shares (see Key 15).

In addition to the mandatory provisions, the articles may contain virtually any lawful provision that is desirable for regulation of the corporation's internal affairs. Such optional provisions might concern preemptive rights, which allow a shareholder to purchase a sufficient number of shares subsequently issued to preserve his or her proportionate interest; quorum requirements for meetings; voting requirements (e.g., each outstanding share is entitled to a single vote unless provided otherwise in the articles); the board's ability to fix compensation; director conflicts of interest; whether board meetings may be held by conference phone; whether the officers and directors are entitled to indemnification from the corporation; how directors may be removed; and so on. Many of these provisions may appear instead in the corporate bylaws. (Note: Pursuant to state law, certain provisions may appear in either the articles or in the bylaws. Generally, it is preferable to place such provisions in the bylaws, since this document is much easier to modify when needed.)

It should be noted that certain objectives cannot be accomplished in the articles. For example, shareholders cannot be excluded from voting on amendment of the articles or on a merger, consolidation, or transfer of all or substantially all of the corporate assets.

If the articles are filed in proper form and are accompanied by the requisite filing fees, the secretary of state is generally required to issue a certificate of incorporation. Should the filing be defective or inadequate, the secretary of state is generally obliged to notify the incorporators of the reason for rejection. In some states, the secretary of state is required either to accept or reject the articles not later than the close of the business day following the day of filing.

Once the certificate of incorporation is issued by the secretary of state's office, corporate existence will generally be reckoned as beginning as of the time of delivery of the articles to the secretary of state. Some states may permit the selection of an alternative date. Note that a *de jure* corporation is formed when there is substantial compliance with all of the mandatory provisions of the incorporation statute; a *de facto* corporation may result if there was a good faith attempt to organize under an incorporation statute; and corporate powers were exercised pursuant to that incorporation, but some defect in connection with the incorporation process prevents it from being a *de jure* corporation. Generally, what constitutes colorable compliance is a matter of state law and involves some effort on the part of the incorporators to prepare and secure the filing of the articles of incorporation. To constitute good faith, the incorporators must not have been aware of the defect when the corporation was organized (see Key 8).

The next step is to prepare for the first official meeting of the incorporators. Generally, the incorporators will execute a waiver of notice of the meeting so that the meeting can be held without delay, unless the proper notice was given. At the first meeting and at all subsequent meetings, minutes must be maintained stating when and where the meeting was held, who was present, and who served as chairperson and as secretary. Generally, the chair first calls the meeting to order and the secretary presents and reads the waiver of notice of the meeting. The chair then reports that the articles were filed in the office of the secretary of state on a specified date and orders that a copy of the certificate of incorporation be inserted in the minute book as part of the official records of the meeting. These are formalities, but they must be followed.

Next, a proposed form of the bylaws for the regulation and management of the affairs of the corporation is read, section by section, and adopted and ordered to be made a part of the permanent records following the certificate of incorporation in the minute book. The board of directors is then elected. As soon as other business is completed, the meeting is adjourned. It is worth mentioning that, subject to state law, a sole incorporator who is also the sole shareholder may file a statement in lieu of holding the organizational meeting.

The next step is to prepare for the initial board of directors meeting. Just as the shareholders did, the directors should execute a waiver of notice of the meeting. Minutes of the board meeting must be maintained, reflecting when and where the meeting was held, who was present, and who served as chairperson and as secretary. Generally, the chair first calls the meeting to order and the secretary presents and reads the waiver of notice of the meeting. Various resolutions are then considered and voted on, such as naming the respective officers; approving the corporate seal and the form of stock certificate; acknowledging who will serve as registered agent and where the corporate bank account will be maintained; authorizing the treasurer to pay all fees and expenses incident to incorporation; accepting the contributions of the various shareholders for their shares; in the case of small corporations, deciding if an S election is desirable; considering possible fringe benefit arrangements, many of which (such as medical reimbursement plans) require corporate action; adopting a fiscal year; designating a principal office location; and such other resolutions and issues as are properly brought before the board. (Note: On occasion, the board will be asked to issue what are known as certified resolutions, which conclusively show to third persons dealing with the corporation that the person acting on behalf of the corporation had the necessary authority. Such resolutions may need to be notarized or placed under seal.) Generally, the directors will then sign a ratification of the minutes, stating that they ratify, approve, and confirm all that transpired at the meeting, the minutes having been read and approved. In lieu of an initial board meeting, it may be possible to take action by the unanimous written consent of the directors.

The corporate bylaws may also be adopted at the initial meeting of the board. Whereas the articles may be viewed as the corporation's "constitution," the bylaws may be seen as internal administrative regulations for carrying on the enterprise. The bylaws cover a broad range of matters, such as the date of the annual meetings, board size, officer authority and duties, board and shareholder meeting notices, places of such meetings, quorum requirements, and indemnification provisions. Although it is possible to include a broad range of items in the bylaws, such provisions must not be inconsistent with the articles or with state law. Further, the power to adopt, alter, or repeal the bylaws following the organizational meeting rests with the board unless the power is reserved exclusively to the shareholders by the articles or in bylaws previously adopted by the shareholders. Since the bylaws are not a matter of public record, like the articles, generally they cannot bind transactions with nonshareholder third parties.

Once the initial directors of the corporation have completed the organizational meeting, shares have been issued, and officers have been elected, the various organizational documents should be placed in a record book, to be updated periodically as meetings are held and other actions are taken. A corporate kit available at many stationery stores provides a handy organizer for a corporation's important records. Some attorneys prefer to keep the corporate records at their law office, but this should be decided by the corporation's officers. Ordinarily, a corporate kit will also include a seal, although many jurisdictions do not require that a seal be used on corporate documents. As a practical matter, many banks continue to require the seal on banking resolutions authorized by the corporation.

As a related matter, much of the data required to be on the face of the share certificates can be engraved thereon by the vendor of the corporate kit. Generally, a share certificate must contain the name of the corporation, a statement that the corporation is organized under the laws of the particular state, the class of shares and the designation of the series (if any) that the certificate represents, the par value of the shares (or a statement that the shares are without par value), and other statements, such as a statement that particular shares are nonvoting. Other required information, including the name of the party to whom the certificate is issued and the number of shares the certificate represents, can be filled in by hand as necessary. The president and corporate secretary will generally need to sign each share certificate.

In some cases, there may be restrictions on the transferability of shares. State and federal securities laws require that a restrictive legend be placed on the certificates representing such shares. These exemptions are generally available for closely held corporations. However, to ensure that these exemptions will be held legal and valid, each shareholder should send an investment letter to the corporation indicating that he or she is purchasing the shares for investment for his own account, acknowledging the restrictions placed on subsequent transfers under federal and state securities law, and agreeing not to transfer the shares in violation of such restrictions. State law may require that a notice of the transaction be filed with the state and a fee paid. The corporate kit will contain not only share certificates but a share transfer ledger, in which can be entered the names of the shareholders, their respective holdings, from whom the shares were transferred, to whom the shares were transferred, and related information. Each subsequent transfer should be reflected in the ledger.

Corporate records should be correctly maintained, and in general the corporation should act like a corporation. Otherwise, creditors may be able to sue the owners individually, and the IRS may attack the separateness of the corporate form. Formal meetings of the board and of the shareholders should be called at least as often as required by state law—and formal minutes should be maintained of all meetings. Moreover, the directors and officers should, in their corporate capacity, make prudent decisions regarding compensation and other matters, and the corporate name should be used at the entrance to the office and on all stationery, contracts, billing, and business forms. Accounting records should be in the name of the corporation, and in no case should the corporate account be comingled with the personal account of the owner(s). Adherence to corporate formalities may seem burdensome at first, but it is absolutely necessary if the corporation is to continue as a viable entity.

Prior to incorporation, it must be determined whether compliance with provisions of the state's Bulk Transfer Act is indicated. By way of background, years ago dishonest sellers often sold out the bulk of their inventory without satisfying unsecured creditors who had extended credit based on the inventory and who were caught off balance, unable to protect their interests. The Uniform Commercial Code, Article 6, requires the *buyer* to notify all creditors—not just those who had relied on the seller's stock in trade in extending credit—of the impending bulk sale. For this purpose, the seller must furnish the buyer with a sworn list of the creditors of the business and usually must file such a list with the clerk of the court. Generally, if the buyer has been given an incomplete list, and thus fails to notify all the creditors of the business, so long as the buyer notifies all of the creditors supplied on the list, the buyer will take the goods free and clear of the claims. (Note: A different result would ensue if the buyer knew or had reason to know that the list furnished was incomplete.) The Bulk Transfer Act generally applies only to the incorporation of existing businesses with inventory and creditors so that the requisite notice must be given to creditors before a buyer can take possession of the goods to be purchased or paid for, whichever comes first. Typically, this statute applies only if there is a sale of the majority of the inventory. Once this requirement has been met, the rules apply to the purchase of equipment as well as inventory.

A new corporation may also apply for a corporate employer identification number, filing Form SS-4 with the IRS, and for the small business electing S corporation status, filing Form 2553 with the IRS. At the state level, application should be made for a sales tax number, since many transactions are subject to the state sales and use tax. In most cases, corporations and other businesses must collect the proper tax on each taxable transaction and periodically forward the money collected to the state. An attorney or accountant generally handles filing these forms.

An attorney may also have to advise whether or not the business will be subject to federal and state unemployment tax. In addition, as far as employees are involved, a number of federal, state, and local laws can be triggered. For example, there are prohibitions against various forms of discrimination; an I-9 Form may need to be completed for the Immigration and Naturalization Service; Occupational Safety and Health Administration (OSHA) regulations must be observed; the Fair Labor

Standards Act (FLSA) includes requirements that covered employees be paid no less than minimum wage and time and one half for hours worked in excess of 40 per week; oppressive child labor practices have been outlawed; and some state right-to-work laws make it unlawful for any person to interfere with the employment of another. Where qualified plans are involved (e.g., pension and profit sharing plans), a host of reporting and disclosure requirements are applicable; fortunately, for plans with fewer than 100 employees, a shorter form may be used.

Most employers are subject to state workers' compensation laws, which impose liability on the employer regardless of fault. A policy should be obtained from an insurer authorized to sell workers' compensation insurance in the state. Other types of insurance are important, too. A business should obtain life insurance on the lives of key employees and perhaps a group life policy as an employee benefit. In order to attract the best employees, a good health insurance program is a must. The business should consider the applicability of property and liability insurance and take a detailed inventory of what assets might be exposed to loss.

The corporation will be required to file federal and, where applicable, state corporate income tax returns. The IRS requires a host of information statements. For example, each year the employer must prepare a Form W-2 for each employee. There are many different 1099 forms that may need to be prepared. Form 1099-MISC is used to report ordinary kinds of payments made, such as rents, royalties, prizes, awards, and nonemployee compensation, whereas Form 1099-INT is used to report payments of interest to a borrower. Every corporation should develop a tax filing schedule to ensure that it is in compliance with all such requirements. The corporation will be required to withhold and pay over income and social security taxes and to pay any applicable intangible personal property tax.

The locality may also impose a tangible personal

property tax, and the state may impose a documentary tax, such as on the transfer of shares. If the firm plans to do business in any states other than the state where it has been incorporated, it may subject itself to penalties if it begins such activity before being authorized to do so by the state.

The corporation will be required to satisfy any zoning or other regulatory requirements and obtain any federal, state, or local licenses. Business licenses may be necessary at both the city and county level. It is important that no contracts or agreements requiring a license be executed until the license or permit is actually obtained. Certain licenses, such as those for the sale of liquor, may require extensive background checks.

Finally, a working knowledge of federal and state securities laws will be useful. Although much of this legislation is more applicable to publicly held corporations, a significant portion of the law does bear on closely held corporations. For example, the governance provisions of the Securities Exchange Act of 1934 apply to corporations with a class of stock registered under Section 12 of that law—this section applies to companies that have at least 500 shareholders of a class of equity securities and more than $5 million in assets. This means that the proxy requirements of Section 14 of the 1934 Act, such as that related to procedures governing how shareholder solicitations are conducted, do not apply to closely held companies. Although proxies are regulated under state law as well, this level of regulation is far less intrusive. Note that whereas the insider trading provisions of the 1934 Act apply to Section 12 companies, Rule 10b-5, which covers much corporate impropriety, applies to transactions in shares of any corporation.

Further, the Securities Act of 1933 applies to the issuance of securities regardless of size. Although exemptions from the registration requirements of the 1933 Act apply to many transactions, a closely held business must study the area carefully.

3

TYPES OF CORPORATIONS

Corporations may be classified in a number of different ways—public or private, profit or nonprofit, publicly held or closely held.

The term *public* has two meanings here. Strictly speaking, public corporations are units of government, such as towns, cities, and villages, and governmental agencies, such as the U.S. Postal Service. In common usage, however, public corporations are those companies in which the general public may own, or purchase, shares of common stock. This stock is generally traded—bought and sold—through a stock exchange or on one of the "over-the-counter" markets.

By far the greatest number of corporations in the United States are closely held, whether within a family or among a limited number of shareholders. Shares are not available to the general public. Most of these enterprises are relatively small in size, although some family companies are very large. For instance, the Hearst Corporation would be in the Fortune 500 if its shares were publicly held.

A form of the closely held corporation that has been under greater scrutiny recently is the S corporation, in which profits are taxed to the shareholders directly. This is not the case in the regular corporation, which generally pays income taxes on its profits before paying dividends to its shareholders, who then must pay income taxes on these distributions. This practice amounts to double taxation, and so Congress authorized the S corporation primarily to relieve small businesses from this extra burden. Another distinction between corporations is their status as profit or nonprofit. The profit category includes all business corporations whether or not they make money in a given year. Indeed, given the risks of starting a small business, many companies that are set up as for-profit corporations never make any money during their entire existence. For the most part the nonprofit category of corporations includes clubs, associations, most schools and colleges, charitable and religious organizations, many cooperatives, and other groups. The officers of nonprofit corporations may or may not be paid a salary, but such corporations may never distribute any surplus funds to directors or members. Most nonprofit corporations do not have any stockholders, but all have a governing body such as a board of directors or trustees. Nonprofits should seek to be tax-qualified such that contributions may be deducted from income for tax purposes and that any corporate earnings will be exempt from taxation.

There are several important distinctions between closely held and publicly held corporations. Although there is no precise definition of what constitutes a closely held (or close or closed or privately held) corporation, generally it is one that is organized in the corporate form and owned and managed by relatively few persons. The "closeness" refers to the relationship of the shareholders, since typically a small group of owners is brought together through family relationships or friendship or mutual business interests. In the case of the publicly held (or public or open) corporation, the shares are owned by a larger, more diverse group and are probably traded either on a securities exchange or over the counter.

Unlike the typical shareholders in a public corporation, who are likely to be simply investors with no intention of assuming any management responsibilities, many shareholders in closely held corporations consider themselves to be active participants in the business. In fact, many such shareholders are employed on a full-time basis by the corporation. The problem is that in the traditional management structure of shareholders, directors, and officers, the corporation, as created by the state, must conform to the statutory norms. This is known as the concession theory and is at odds with the practical reality of the closely held corporation, in which shareholders may wish to agree among themselves as to how the business will be managed.

Depending on the law in one's state of incorporation, close corporations may be subject to the general incorporation law or to specially drafted statutes designed to deal with their particular concerns. Thus, under California law, a corporation with 10 or fewer shareholders can elect close corporation status so that it can operate more or less as an incorporated partnership under a shareholders agreement, dispensing with many of the corporate formalities. Under Delaware law, the stock of such a close corporation may not be held by more than 30 persons. Additional restrictions are that the corporation's stock will be subject to restraints on transferability and that the corporation will make no public offering of its securities.

California law also holds that "the failure of a close corporation to observe corporate formalities relating to meetings of directors or shareholders in connection with the management of its affairs, pursuant to an agreement...shall not be considered a factor tending to establish that the shareholders have personal liability for corporate obligations." Although operating on such an informal basis will not subject the shareholders to personal liability for corporate debts, shareholders who assume management responsibility may be subject to liability for management acts or omissions that would otherwise be imposed on directors. In other words, an owner-manager has responsibilities similar to those of a director in a publicly held corporation. Note further that close-corporation statutes vary considerably in terms of the arrangements offered, from enabling shareholders to replace directors by assuming some or all of the management powers, to allowing a majority of the shareholders to enter into an enforceable management agreement, to enabling the shareholders to enter into agreements modifying the basic structure and rights of the corporation as to resemble a partnership, to allowing a shareholder (or at least those owning a specified percentage of shares) to force the corporation's legal termination.

The idea of such shareholder agreements is to enable the shareholders to provide for any system of management and control they want. Such a comprehensive agreement may cover such basic matters as employment rights, management and voting rights, deadlock and dissolution, and the transferability of shares. For example, a corporation's continued eligibility as an S corporation may be jeopardized if a transfer is made to an ineligible shareholder. By entering into such an agreement, a corporation's risk should be minimized. The actual agreement may appear in the articles of incorporation or the bylaws—or they may be freestanding (i.e., contained in a separate document), depending on state law and/or the parties involved. In some states, certain kinds of agreements will be permitted only if they have been included in the articles. In any case, notice of the existence of an agreement should be placed on the stock certificates held by the parties to the agreement. In some states, even a minority of shareholders may enter into such agreements, whereas other laws offer greater support if all of the shareholders are parties. Even in states where the statutes require that the agreement be located in the articles, some courts have enforced such understandings in unanimous agreements that were not so included.

In terms of the contents of such agreements, they vary widely but often provide for greater-than-majority quorum and voting requirements for both shareholder and board meetings. Such requirements effectively give the minority interests a veto power, which is something akin to the unanimity requirements associated with the partnership form. One might ask why a majority interest would give a minority shareholder such power over corporate affairs. The answer is that power sharing might be necessary in order to attract individuals who might not otherwise participate in the venture. In other cases, an agreement can bring together two or more minority shareholders who together constitute a majority and who wish to ensure that the contracting parties will continue to act together in the future.

Although many of the principles that are applicable to corporations generally (e.g., matters of corporate finance) do apply to the closely held corporation, the operation of most close corporations resembles more closely the partnership form. Like a partnership, the relationship among the owners must be one of confidence and utmost loyalty. Although courts are looking more closely to determine if majority interests have oppressed the minority shareholders (e.g., by unreasonably withholding dividends), this is not basically the answer. Taking preventive measures, such as inserting provisions for the rights of minority shareholders in the articles of incorporation, offers a much broader guarantee.

As far as publicly held corporations are concerned, with the exception of those who own a controlling interest in a business, the powers of the shareholders are limited to the election of directors, the adoption, amendment, or repeal of the bylaws, and the consideration of certain fundamental changes in the corporate structure. Although shareholders may also vote in other specialized actions—such as approving contracts involving interested directors, authorizing indemnification of directors and officers, and authorizing loans to officers—and become involved in some aspects of corporate oversight such as inspecting the corporate books and records under specified circumstances, it is truly the board that actually exercises the corporate powers and is responsible for the management of the business.

In reality, then, both closely held and publicly held

corporations may sell shares to raise funds, but shareholders in the former generally participate directly in management, whereas shareholders in the latter generally leave the management of the business to others. Not surprisingly, therefore, publicly held corporations are subject to a much greater degree of scrutiny concerning their affairs than are closely held corporations.

4

CORPORATE
LOCATION AND NAME

One of the first questions prospective incorporators must answer is: In what state shall we incorporate and under what name? As a general rule, a business should be incorporated in the state where its principal place of operation is located. The possible advantages of filing for incorporation outside one's home jurisdiction (e.g., more favorable taxes or laws, simpler procedures, and less pervasive governmental supervision) typically will be outweighed by the extra cost and trouble associated with out-of-state incorporation.

Although certain states like Delaware have gained a well-deserved reputation as being receptive to the changing needs of business, most states today do offer a modern corporation statute that does not place unreasonable restrictions on operations (be they small business or otherwise). Of course, small businesses located in a metropolitan area that encompasses two or more states might find it worthwhile to investigate the laws in each state. This would be particularly true of a retailer or other business operating in more than one state.

Differences in corporate law among states range from the trivial to the significant. Thus, the states vary as to whether the incorporators must subscribe to stock, and if so, for how much, how many persons must serve as incorporators, and whether partnerships and corporations may themselves act as incorporators. Some states require that a director be a U.S. citizen, and in some states directors must also be shareholders. In some states, directors may be indemnified under the articles, bylaws, or other corporate provisions, whereas in other states, the indemnification statute is deemed exclusive. In some states, a majority of the directors constitutes a quorum unless the articles or bylaws provide otherwise, whereas in other states, a quorum may be less than a majority but not less than one third (or at least two thirds) of the total directors. Other states don't mandate such a minimum.

States also vary as to the number of directors required. If there is only one shareholder, state law may authorize a one-person board. But some states require that there be more than one incorporator and director. This makes such states unappealing to entrepreneurs, who prefer to keep initial control of the corporation in their own hands. Under the RMBCA, the number of directors may be specified or fixed in accordance with the articles or bylaws. In terms of voting, state laws vary widely. Thus, in some jurisdictions, the right to vote cannot be denied to any class of shares, making it impossible to create nonvoting stock as a means of preserving control. There also may be requirements that set a minimum paid-in capital, and some states provide that par value of the shares may not be less than $1 each. Should a corporation begin doing business before the minimum has been paid in, liability may attach for the difference between the minimum paid-in capital and the amount actually paid in. As far as stock that is issued without par value is concerned, some jurisdictions arbitrarily evaluate no-par for initial tax purposes at $10 to $100 per share, whereas others do not even authorize the use of no-par shares.

These are but a few of the variations that exist among the states. A detailed analysis of the various state laws and cases decided thereunder can be found in the *Model Business Corporation Act Annotated*, which is available in many county law libraries.

At one point in time an important reason for incorporating in a state other than the true home state was to avoid service of process, or being subject to legal action. Some businesspeople without legal experience still believe that in most cases people won't bother to sue or to take other legal action if they have to go out of state to do so. But this is no longer true, because this advantage has been substantially eliminated through the adoption of the so-called long-arm statutes, which effectively permit the courts to exercise jurisdiction on the basis of a variety of corporate actions within the state, such as the commencement of a tort, the making of a contract, or the ownership of property.

As regards location, consideration should also be given to any applicable taxes and fees, the business climate, and the relevant case law. To cite an example of one state's structure, under Pennsylvania law, two types of state corporate income taxes are imposed. There is a corporate net income tax, referred to as an excise tax, and a corporation income tax, essentially a property tax levied on corporations that are not subject to the corporate net income tax but that own property or conduct activities in the state. Then there is the state capital stock tax and a franchise tax. Certain types of entities, such as banks, are exempted. Pennsylvania also has a corporate loans tax.

It is worth noting that state corporate income and other taxes may even be assessed on out-of-state corporations so long as such taxation does not discriminate against companies engaged in interstate commerce, does not "unduly burden" interstate commerce, and does not violate a corporation's right to due process. The taxes or fees must serve a legitimate interest of the state imposing them, and be reasonable in relation to the corporation's activity within the state.

So much for location. Choosing a name for your corporation is generally simple enough. Of course, there are some practical considerations, such as the appropriateness of the name to the business, its advertising potential, and its availability and protectability. Subject to state law, each name must contain the word "corporation", "incorporated", "limited", or an abbreviated version thereof to indicate that an entity is incorporated. Some states also recognize the use of "company" or "co." as a sufficient indication of corporate status.

After a name has been selected, it must be approved by the state. Here there may be some unforeseen problems, because the name may not lawfully be the same as that of another corporation already formed or qualified to do business in the state. Interestingly, the old version of the Model Business Corporation Act did not allow a name that was the same as, or deceptively similar to, any other corporate name—and that is still the law in many states. The Revised Act (RMBCA) requires only that the name be distinguishable upon the records of the secretary of state from any other corporate name. Relatedly, insofar as out-of-state business operations are concerned, generally no application for authority to transact business in a state may be issued to a corporation unless its name conforms to law.

How can one determine whether a particular name is available? Generally, the secretary of state's office stores corporate names in a computer that provides immediate access. Subject to state law, name availability can be determined over the counter in the secretary of state's office, by written correspondence, or sometimes over the phone. There may be a charge for checking availability after the first name. There are private companies that can handle this and other parts of the incorporating process. They are often listed in the Yellow Pages under incorporating companies. Typically, an attorney handling an incorporation will ask for a first, second, and a third choice in order of preference. The most prudent will also check other sources, since the secretary of state's approval of a name does not protect against a claim that a name's use amounts to a trademark infringement or unfair competition.

Once it is determined that a name is available, it should be reserved. Reservation is especially important if the articles of incorporation are not going to be drafted, executed, and filed soon after availability of the name is established. Anyone intending to form a corporation may reserve a name. The application generally must set forth the name and address of the applicant, the name to be reserved, and the date of reservation. If the secretary of state finds that the name applied for is still available, the name generally will be reserved for a non-renewable period (e.g., 120 days).

There are some additional considerations. In many states, it is forbidden to include in the corporate name such words as *insurance* and *bank* unless their use is explicitly permitted by law. The reason is that such firms are regulated by the state so that special licenses—or approvals—are necessary for a corporation to operate in such fields. Further, many corporations will do business under a name that is not the same as the name in the articles. Fictitious-name statutes make it unlawful to do business under such a name without providing public notice of intention to use the name and registering it by filing an affidavit with the clerk of the county where the principal place of business is to be located or with the secretary of state's office.

You will need proof of publication of the fictitious name when you open your corporate bank account. The bank will also want to see the articles of incorporation, the corporate seal, employer identification number (or proof that the tax number has been applied for), and of course any corporate resolution authorizing the account. The latter is generally on a bank-provided form. (Caveat: The bank may impose a penalty if the tax number is not obtained in a specified period, e.g., 60 days). Importantly, in some states, like Florida, anyone failing to comply with the DBA ("doing business as") statute may not maintain a suit in a court of law until the requirement has been satisified.

In sum, the selected corporate name should not be so similar to the name of an existing corporation or other business entity that it could result in deception, unfair competition, or confusion. Once the name has been selected, it may be changed by amendment of the articles of incorporation. The change of the corporate name will have no effect on the corporation's obligations or property rights, however. Thus, the corporate existence will continue unchanged.

5

CORPORATE PURPOSES AND POWERS

Most corporations operate under a charter granted by a state. Included in that charter is a statement of purpose, written by the incorporators and approved by the state. In addition, corporations operate under state law, which grants them certain powers and restricts them in certain areas.

Corporate Purposes. Under the RMBCA, every corporation has the purpose of engaging in any lawful business, unless a more limited purpose is set forth in the articles. The RMBCA also provides that a corporation engaging in a business that is subject to regulation under another statute (e.g., banking), may incorporate under the RMBCA only if permitted by such other statute.

Many incorporators have found it useful to set forth a statement of purpose that includes a brief description of the activities their corporation will engage in.

For example, a retail store might have purposes similar to the following:

"To manufacture, produce, purchase, or otherwise acquire, sell, import, export, distribute, and deal in goods, wares, merchandise and materials of any kind and description."

In addition to this specific list of purposes, there might be a paragraph such as the following, which leaves the door open to other business opportunities:

"The foregoing purposes and activities will be interpreted as examples only and not as limitations, and nothing here shall be deemed as prohibiting the corporation from extending its activities to any related or otherwise permissible lawful business purposes which may become necessary, profitable, or desirable for the furtherance of the corporate objectives expressed above."

The rationale for the broadly worded purposes clause is that it permits a corporation to take advantage of any opportunity when action must be taken quickly.

Related to the issue of corporate purpose is that of corporate powers. Under the RMBCA, unless the articles provide otherwise, every corporation will have perpetual duration and succession in its corporate name and the same powers as an individual to do all things necessary or convenient to carry out its business and affairs, including without limitation the following powers:

1. To sue and be sued, complain, and defend itself in its corporate name.
2. To have a corporate seal, which may be altered at will.
3. To make and amend bylaws, not inconsistent with its articles of incorporation or with the laws of the state, for managing the business and regulating the affairs of the corporation.
4. To purchase, receive, lease, or otherwise acquire, and own, hold, improve, use, and otherwise deal with, real or personal property, or any legal or equitable interest in property, wherever located.
5. To sell, convey, mortgage, pledge, lease, exchange, and otherwise dispose of all or any part of the property.
6. To purchase, receive, subscribe for, or otherwise acquire; own, hold, vote, use, sell, mortgage, lend, pledge, or otherwise dispose of; and deal in and with shares or other interests in, or obligations of, any other entity.
7. To make contracts and guarantees, incur liabilities, borrow money, issue its notes, bonds, and other obli-

gations, and secure any obligations by mortgage or pledge of any of its property, franchises, or income.

8. To lend money, invest, and reinvest its funds, and receive and hold real and personal property as security for repayment.

9. To be a promoter, partner, member, associate, or manager of any partnership, joint venture, trust, or other entity.

10. To conduct its business, locate offices, and exercise the powers granted by law within or without the state.

11. To elect directors and appoint officers, employees, and agents of the corporation, define their duties, fix their compensation, and lend them money and credit.

12. To pay pensions and establish pension plans, pension trusts, profit-sharing plans, share bonus plans, share option plans, and benefit or incentive plans for any or all current or former directors, officers, employees, and agents.

13. To make donations for the public welfare or for charitable, scientific, or educational purposes.

14. To transact any lawful business that will aid governmental policy.

15. To make payments or donations, or do any other act, not inconsistent with law, that furthers the business and affairs of the corporation.

Beyond these general powers, there are so-called emergency powers. Further, a corporation generally has all powers necessary or convenient to effect any or all of the purposes for which the corporation was formed. This is known as *residual* power.

Some terminology would be useful here. An *intra vires* act is one within the powers of the corporation. An *ultra vires* act is one beyond the corporate powers. At common law, when a corporation has entered into an *ultra vires* contract, either the corporation or a third party with whom it contracted could disaffirm the contract, since the corporation lacked capacity to enter into the contract. More recently, courts have tended to use the doctrine of ratification to validate an otherwise *ultra vires* contract so long as there was unanimous shareholder approval.

Under the RMBCA, the validity of a corporate act may not be challenged on the ground that the corporation lacked power except in a proceeding by a shareholder against the corporation to enjoin the act, in a proceeding by the corporation through a receiver, trustee, or other legal representative against an incumbent or former director, officer, employee, or agent of the corporation, or in a proceeding by the state attorney general. For example, a misuse of corporate assets by an officer for personal purposes constitutes a breach of fiduciary duty and may be enjoined, but is not necessarily considered an *ultra vires* act. In sum, most corporate articles now track the language of local corporate statutes empowering the corporation to engage in "any lawful business." Such provisions effectively preclude any conceivable challenge that the corporation acted beyond its powers of incorporation.

Before leaving the subject of corporate powers, three issues are worth addressing. First, older laws did not expressly empower corporations to enter into partnerships. Modern statutes do so; corporations may now serve as partners. Next, since the object of a for-profit enterprise is to conduct business with a view to making a profit, at one point it was unclear whether corporations could make donations for charitable purposes. Today, many statutes explicitly confer upon corporations the power to make donations for such purposes, although this power, like other powers, is subject to an implied limit of reasonableness. Finally, older laws did not expressly confer upon corporations the power to guarantee the debts of others. Modern statutes do so; thus, a corporation can make contracts of suretyship or guaranty, but such power can generally be exercised only in furtherance of the corporate business.

6

FILING THE ARTICLES OF INCORPORATION

Generally, a corporation is organized by the execution and filing of the corporate charter, which is known as the articles of incorporation or, simply, the articles, along with any required filing fees and registry statement. The individuals who form the corporation are known as incorporators. Depending on state law, the incorporators may be required to file a registry statement for informational purposes. Basically, in this document the incorporators set forth the name of the corporation, an address to which correspondence may be directed, the statutory authority under which the business was incorporated, the kinds of businesses to be transacted, and other information as may be required by law.

Among the other duties of the incorporators are signing the articles, delivering them to the secretary of state or other official, and executing the registry statement. A number of states permit one person to serve as incorporator and/or permit a corporation to serve as the incorporator.

As to what must be contained in the articles, some states have prescribed forms for this purpose, whereas others allow considerable flexibility. Under the RMBCA, the articles must set forth a corporate name, the number of shares that the corporation is authorized to issue, the street address of the initial registered office, the name of the registered agent to accept service of process, and the name and address of each incorporator. Under the RMBCA, the articles may also set forth the following:

1. The names and addresses of the individuals who are to serve as the initial directors.
2. Provisions not inconsistent with law regarding:
   a. the purpose or purposes for which the corporation is organized;
   b. managing the business and regulating the affairs of the corporation;
   c. defining, limiting, and regulating the powers of the corporation, its board of directors, and shareholders;
   d. a par value for authorized shares or classes of shares;
   e. the imposition of personal liability on shareholders for debts of the corporation to a specified extent and upon specified conditions.
3. Any provision required by law or permitted to be set forth in the bylaws.

The articles may cover many other points as well, such as establishing preemptive rights and transfer restrictions, allowing for cumulative voting, and calling for special meetings. If all the documents are in order, the secretary of state will approve the articles, file the original, and return a certified copy of the articles and a receipt to the incorporators. (In some states, the secretary may just mark the copies to show that the articles have been filed and endorsed with the required approval.) It may be necessary to make sure that a certified copy of the articles is recorded in the office of the clerk of the county in which the corporation will do business, own real estate, or maintain its principal office. Some states and localities have additional requirements.

Note that the secretary of state merely reviews the incorporation documents to determine if they comply with the filing requirements of the state. The secretary of state's office does not review the documents for such matters as corporate governance and capitalization, compliance with other business or regulatory laws, or tax status. Thus, in certain instances where the wording of one or more provisions is important, an attorney should be consulted to ensure that the articles have been drawn properly. For example, in order for a nonprofit corporation to qualify as such for federal tax purposes, the corporate purposes and other sections must conform with federal tax laws.

Unless a delayed effective date is specified, the corporate existence generally begins when the articles are filed. Under the RMBCA, the secretary of state's filing of the articles is conclusive proof that the incorporators have satisfied all conditions precedent to incorporation, except in a proceeding by the state to cancel or revoke the incorporation or to involuntarily dissolve the corporation.

After the articles are filed, the incorporators or the board of directors named in the articles hold a meeting to complete the corporate organization. Subject to state law, such a meeting may be held within or outside the state. This meeting is held in the same manner as other meetings of stockholders or directors. In setting up the articles, incorporators may specify procedures for voting, such as a supermajority for the adoption of important measures. It is not a good idea to require a unanimous vote, even on the most important issues, since that can be difficult to achieve. In such instances it might be preferable to require the unanimous vote of the quorum actually present.

At the initial meeting, the articles are ordered into the record of the meeting and the bylaws adopted, or a committee is appointed to draft them. Under the RMBCA, the bylaws may contain any provision for managing the business and regulating the affairs of the corporation that is not inconsistent with state law. If any restrictions on the power of the directors are set forth in the articles, third parties are bound by them. Restrictions that are only in the bylaws, however, are not binding on third parties, since the bylaws are not filed and made a matter of public record.

7

TAX ASPECTS OF FORMING A CORPORATION

When a taxpayer transfers property in exchange for other property, there is normally a gain or a loss. Such gain or loss is computed by comparing the adjusted basis, or cost, of the property given up with the value of the property received. This realized gain or loss must be recognized for tax purposes unless a particular exception applies.

Under Section 351 of the tax law, if one or more persons transfer property to a corporation solely in exchange for stock or securities, and the transferors, taken as a group, are in control of the corporation immediately after the exchange, the transferors will not recognize gain or loss in the exchange. Thus, in the normal course of events, owners of a business who decide to incorporate will not have to pay any income tax based on the transaction. The theory is that such transfers represent mere changes in form and thus should not be recognized until an economically significant event occurs. The same principle applies not only to transfers to new corporations but to existing corporations as well.

Section 351 is very important for closely held corporations, most of which should be eligible for the benefits of this provision. Note, however, that all such shareholders are required to file a statement with their federal income tax returns providing details as to the exchange. In effect, Section 351 is a deferral provision. Thus, it merely postpones the day that the realized gain or loss will be recognized. One might ask why a shareholder might ever opt out of Section 351. If, however, a transferor wishes to recognize a realized loss, has a capital loss or a net operating loss carryover to offset the gain, or desires to take a stepped-up basis in assets transferred, the transferor might decide on a taxable incorporation. This goal can be accomplished either by a sale to the corporation—a sale of assets for cash—or the failure to meet one of the requirements of Section 351, such as the control test, as spelled out below.

For the purposes defined in Section 351, a *person* includes not only individuals, but estates, trusts, partnerships, associations, companies, and corporations. The term *property* includes not only money, realty, personal property, and intangibles, but also such items as patents and patentable know-how. Thus, secret processes and formulas, along with proprietary information in the general nature of patentable inventory, qualify as property under Section 351. However, property does not encompass services—whether past, present, or future—so the distinction between past services and know-how, which *is* property for tax purposes, is important. Further, transferors of services who also transfer property to the corporation in exchange for stock or other securities will include the securities received for services in determining whether the control requirement (described below) is satisfied. Since the law seeks to prevent nominal transfers by existing stockholders in order to qualify someone else's exchange as tax-free, the transferred property must not be of a relatively small value compared with the stock already owned or to be received in exchange for services. As a rule of thumb, the IRS generally will not consider property to be of a relatively small value if the fair market value of the property transferred equals at least 10 percent of the fair market value of the stock or securities already owned by the transferor or to be received in exchange for services by the transferor.

Stock includes all shares—be they voting or nonvoting,

common or preferred—but excludes stock rights and warrants; securities refer to all debt with the exception of short-term notes. The reason is that the nonrecognition sections—including Section 351—are designed to permit the tax-free transfer of property only if the transfer is not analogous to a sale. The problem with short-term notes is their close resemblance to cash as distinct from an ongoing interest in the corporation. Although what constitutes a short-term note is not free from doubt, generally, notes with terms of five years or less will not qualify as securities.

It was noted earlier that for Section 351 to apply, the transferors must be in control of the corporation immediately after the exchange. The control test is taken from the reorganization area of the Internal Revenue Code. For this purpose, control means ownership of at least 80 percent of the total combined voting power of all classes of stock entitled to vote and ownership of at least 80 percent of the total number of shares of all other classes of stock. Note that if two or more classes of voting stock are issued, the transferors must take back shares possessing 80 percent or more of the *total* voting power, regardless of the number of shares in each class. However, if two or more classes of nonvoting stock are issued, the transferors must receive at least 80 percent of the number of shares in each class of nonvoting stock.

The test for control requirement is the interest that the transferors *as a group* receive in the corporation. Thus, if Thatcher and Hatcher each transfer property for 50 percent of the shares of the business, the control requirement would be satisfied even though neither person individually winds up with the required control. Note, however, that the stock ownership must be actual, since the attribution-of-ownership rules do not apply here. Thus, if husband, wife, and son each own a third of the shares of a corporation and only husband and son transfer property to the corporation in exchange for securities, the transaction will not qualify under Section 351 because the transferors (husband and son) will not be 80 percent "in control" immediately after the exchange.

"Immediately after the exchange" does not mean an instantaneous transfer is required, so if control is achieved as a result of a series of planned transactions, the requirements would be met. Thus, if the rights of the parties have been defined prior to the exchange and the execution of the plan follows ordinary procedure, the exchange should qualify as being tax-free. Note that a formalized agreement among the parties is not normally required—just a general plan among the parties that contemplates the transfer by several persons of specified cash and other property so as to unite the transferors into the requisite group.

A recurring issue in the Section 351 area concerns the receipt of so-called boot. If a transferor receives not only stock or securities in the swap but some other property or cash "to boot," any gain is recognized but only to the extent of the fair market value of the boot received. Losses are still not recognized. The assumption of a liability or the acquisition of property subject to a liability is not treated as boot, except to the extent that the liability assumed or taken subject to the asset exceeds the transferor's adjusted basis in the transferred property. The IRS has contended that the transfer of property subject to a liability results in gain to the extent of the excess over basis, whether or not the transferee could be expected to pay the liability. Note that the transferee corporation receives a basis equal to the transferor's adjusted basis, increased by the gain recognized by the transferor. In 1999, however, the rule that a liability was automatically treated as assumed where property was taken subject to it was repealed. Now, only liabilities that are treated as assumed result in a basis increase to the transferee corporation. A *recourse liability* is treated as assumed if, on the basis of all the facts and circumstances, the transferee agreed to, and is expected to, satisfy the liability, or a portion thereof, whether or not the transferor has been relieved of the liability. A *nonrecourse liability* is treated as assumed by the transferee of any asset subject to the liability, except that the amount of nonrecourse liability treated as assumed is reduced by the lesser of: (1) the portion of the debt to be paid by another party, or (2) the fair market value of the other assets subject to the liability. To the extent that gain is recognized by the transferor as a result of an assumption of a liability by a transferee corporation, the transferee's basis may not be increased above the property's fair market value. (Note: Under the Taxpayer Relief Act of 1997, certain kinds of nonqualified preferred stock are treated as boot as well.)

Assuming that a transferor transfers property in exchange for stock or securities under Section 351, the transferor's basis in the stock and securities received is generally the same as the basis in the property given up. Such basis is decreased by the sum of any boot received as well as the transferor's debt the corporation assumes or takes subject to, and is increased by any gain recognized in the exchange. The stock is a capital asset in the hands of the transferor even if the assets transferred were not.

Let's take an example. If Thatcher transfers property with a fair market value of $100 and a basis to her of $40 in a Section 351 exchange, her basis in the stock and securities received will still be $40. Since the transaction qualifies as a tax-free exchange under Section 351, the gain inherent in the assets is deferred, and the transferor takes a carryover basis in the stock equal to his or her basis in the assets transferred. The gain is recognized later if the stock is sold. However, if Thatcher receives stock with a fair market value of $70 and $30 in boot, she will recognize gain of $30, and her basis in the stock will be $40. Note that a transferor who takes more than one class of stock and securities must allocate his or her basis among them according to their relative fair market values.

So much for the transferor. The corporation's basis in the assets it receives is the same as their basis in the hands of the transferor, increased by any gain the transferor-shareholder recognized in the exchange. This carryover of basis applies to each item of property so that no reallocation is necessary among the property received by the corporation unless gain has been recognized by the transferor. Note that the tax status of these assets to the corporation—as capital assets, depreciable business property, and so on—depends on how they are used by the corporation, irrespective of the status they had with the transferor, but the corporation's holding period includes the transferor's holding period. As far as the shareholder is concerned, the holding period of stock received by the shareholder in a Section 351 tax-free exchange includes the shareholder's holding period for the property transferred, if the property was either a capital asset or real or depreciable property used in a business and held for more than 12 months. The holding period of stock received by the stockholder in exchange for inventory, or other items held for sale to customers in the ordinary course of a trade or business, begins the day the stock is received. As noted, however, the corporation's holding period for property received in an exchange includes the holding period of the transferor. Also note: At the request of interested parties, the IRS will rule in advance of a proposed incorporation as to whether the shareholders will receive the desired tax treatment (see Rev. Proc. 81-57, 1981-2 CB 674).

There are a number of other issues associated with corporation formation. For example, organizational costs incurred in forming the corporate entity are treated as costs associated with the creation of a capital asset and therefore are not deductible when paid or accrued, but are amortizable over a period of not less than 60 months beginning with the month in which the corporation begins business. To qualify as an organizational cost, the expense must be incident to the creation of the corporation, chargeable to the capital account of the corporation, and of a character that, if expended incident to the creation of a corporation having a limited life, would be amortizable over such life. Examples include fees paid to the state of incorporation, expenses of temporary directors, and legal and accounting fees resulting from organizing the corporation. Organizational costs should be distinguished from start-up costs, which also are not currently deductible but are amortized over a period of not less than 60 months, starting with the month in which the active trade or business began. Start-up costs must meet two criteria: they must be paid or incurred in connection with the investigation, acquisition, or creation of an active trade or business, and they must be of the same nature as an expense that would be currently deductible if paid or incurred in connection with the expansion of an existing trade or business in the same field.

The foregoing discussion relates to federal tax aspects associated with corporate formation. Generally, the states do have an exemption from the sales tax for transfers to a corporation in exchange for the corporation's stock. However, these exemptions must be examined carefully. For example, New York exempts transfers when the corporation is organized but taxes subsequent transfers. States like Georgia exempt the transfer only if the transferor has the same proportionate interest in the asset after the transfer; other states make a distinction according to the consideration received. Be sure to consult your tax adviser in this regard.

Note that professional service corporations frequently have substantial accounts receivable. Generally, on formation of the new corporation, accounts receivable and payable will be transferred to the corporation. If the proprietorship or partnership was on the cash basis method of accounting—charging off specific accounts receivable as they became worthless rather than setting up a bad debt reserve, and deducting business expenses as they accrued—no particular tax problem would ordinarily arise. However, if the business employed an accrual method with a reserve for bad debts, potential tax problems arise that should be explored with an accountant or other tax adviser.

8

DE FACTO AND
DE JURE
CORPORATIONS

After the articles of incorporation have been filed and any required fees paid, a question may arise as to when corporate existence begins. This, too, varies according to state law. Under Florida law, for instance, commencement of corporate existence, if specified in the articles, may occur up to five days before or 90 days after filing. Under the RMBCA, unless a delayed effective date is specified, corporate existence begins when the articles are filed. The RMBCA also provides that filing with the secretary of state is conclusive proof that the incorporators have satisfied all of the conditions for incorporation.

***De Jure* Corporations.** Sometimes the state may move to cancel or to revoke the incorporation or to dissolve the corporation. If there is a defect in the incorporation process, the question arises as to whether the corporate identity is to be respected. If there is at least substantial compliance with the state's law, the corporation will be deemed to have *de jure* status. In this case, the corporation may not be attacked by the state or by a third party (such as a creditor trying to reach a shareholder directly). Note that perfect compliance with state law is not necessary, just substantial compliance. Thus, there ordinarily must be compliance with all mandatory provisions of the law in order to qualify for *de jure* status. Words like "must", tend to indicate a mandatory provision, whereas words like "may" tend to evidence what is called a directory provision.

De Facto **Corporations.** In some cases there may have been a "colorable attempt in good faith" to organize a corporation pursuant to law, but some defect in the incorporation process has prevented classification as a *de jure* corporation. If the corporation has exercised corporate powers such as issuing stock or electing directors, it should have the same status as a *de jure* corporation to enter into contracts. Such a corporation is called a *de facto* corporation, and only the state through the attorney general's office may attack its validity. The procedure used by the state for this purpose is called a *quo warranto* proceeding, in which the state essentially asks, "By what warrant or authority does the corporation exist?"

In effect, a *de facto* corporation is treated as a valid corporation with respect to third parties. Thus, it is important to understand the elements of the *de facto* doctrine. Although what constitutes a "colorable attempt" at compliance is not totally clear, it generally involves an effort to prepare and file the articles. As to what constitutes "in good faith," it generally means that the shareholders raising the defense of *de facto* status were not aware of the organizational defects when they ran the business.

Other Alternatives. Should the organizational procedures not give rise to either a *de jure* or a *de facto* corporation—for example, if no powers were ever exercised by the corporation—even third parties may attack its existence. In such cases, the shareholders may be held individually liable, although even here courts have split on the question of whether all shareholders should be held responsible or just those who actively participated in the management of the business.

9

LIMITED LIABILITY

As noted previously, the seminal advantage of the corporate form is the limited liability it offers shareholders. The basic premise is that corporate creditors are not permitted to satisfy corporate debts by suing or otherwise going against the shareholders. In fact, if the owners are personally liable for all the debts of the business, the entity is not a corporation.

When an existing business is incorporated, the former owners of the business continue to be liable to creditors of the old business for taxes and debts incurred prior to incorporation, unless the owners have been released from this liability. In the case of incorporation of a partnership, subject to state law, the former partners may be held liable for debts incurred after incorporation if it is determined that the creditor was not notified of the dissolution of the partnership.

Sole proprietors and general partners have unlimited personal liability in all obligations of the business. However, it is useful to compare the status of a limited partner in a limited partnership with the liability of a corporate shareholder. The liability of a limited partner is limited to the amount of his or her capital contribution unless the partner takes part in the management of the business, in which case he or she may assume personal liability. On the other hand, the shareholder of a corporation may participate fully in the operations of the business without incurring personal liability for the debts and obligations of the business. As a practical matter, though, for a new enterprise, banks and some other lenders may require personal guarantees from the shareholders as a means of ensuring payment. However, certain creditors such as trade creditors do not typically require such assurances so long as the business is a going concern and there is no marked impairment of credit.

Another recurring question is whether insolvency of the corporation will absolve the owners of tax obligations, especially for employment tax. Classically, a troubled corporation has creditors who are pressing it for payment. Meanwhile, it holds employment taxes that it is obligated to pay over to the government. The federal tax code levies a significant penalty against corporate officers and other "responsible persons" for failure to withhold and pay over such taxes, and the government will go after such individuals personally. "Responsible persons" are defined as those who have the duty to perform or the power to direct the act of collecting, accounting for, or paying over trust fund moneys. At issue, then, is which party was under a duty to see to it that taxes were withheld, collected, or paid over to the government as of the specific time that the failure to withhold, collect, or pay over the taxes occurred. Of course, such failure must be "willful," which basically means intentional, deliberate, voluntary, and knowing, as distinguished from accidental. In any case, it is important not to use such earmarked funds for other purposes. A similar problem can arise in respect to unpaid wages, which can subject corporate officers to civil and/or criminal sanctions depending on state law. Likewise, some jurisdictions hold corporate officers liable if the corporation has not made required payments under the unemployment compensation law.

Illegal Dividends. The basic question in this area is whether directors can be found liable for their actions, thus negating limited liability. For instance, if the board of directors declares an illegal dividend, the directors will be jointly and severally liable to the corporation for the benefit of creditors or preferred shareholders who were affected by the dividend. In states that follow the original MBCA, the corporation can collect the full amount of this "illegal" dividend. Many jurisdictions, however, limit recovery to the amount of the injury suffered, which is basically the amount owed to the creditors and the amount by which the illegal dividend impaired preferences of the preferred shares. Further, modern statutes tend to protect directors from liability when they relied in good faith on the books of the corporation.

It should be noted that shareholders as well as directors may be personally liable for illegal dividends. Generally, in insolvent corporations, each shareholder who received a dividend will be required to return it to the corporation for the benefit of creditors and the preferred shareholders. Shareholders in solvent corporations are generally permitted to keep an illegal distribution, assuming that they received it in good faith (i.e., they did not know that the dividend came from an improper source). Of course, if the shareholder knew of the illegal source of the dividends, or can be charged with such knowledge, a different result may ensue.

Before leaving the subject of limited liability, it might be useful to briefly discuss a new form of entity available in many states, known as the limited liability company. This entity qualifies for federal tax purposes as a partnership while protecting owners and managers from liability. Thus, like a limited partnership, members of a limited liability company have no personal liability for the obligations of the enterprise. Unlike a limited partnership, members here can participate directly in the management of the business. Unlike an S corporation, there are no restrictions on the number or type of owners, and, in allocating profits and losses, the limited liability company has all the flexibility of a partnership whereas an S corporation can issue only one class of stock. If a limited liability company is classified as a partnership for federal tax purposes, it will be subject to tax under Subchapter K of the Internal Revenue Code. The company will not be subject to tax at the corporate level, with its income, gain, loss, deductions, and credits passing through and taxed directly to the members in accordance with their distributive shares. The member's tax basis in his or her limited liability interest will generally equal the amount of money and the adjusted basis of property contributed by the member, and his or her share of the company's liabilities.

The share of liabilities depends on whether the company's liabilities are recourse or nonrecourse. A liability is considered recourse to the extent that any member bears the economic risk of loss (e.g., by guaranteeing the company's debt). The member's share of the recourse liabilities equals the portion of such liabilities for which that member bears the economic risk of loss. A company's liabilities are nonrecourse if no member bears the economic risk of loss. Nonrecourse debt is allocated among all members. Most liabilities will be nonrecourse, because the members of the limited liability company are not liable for the debts of the company and do not wish to make themselves subject to such debts. In any event, a member of a limited liability company may not deduct any losses in excess of the adjusted basis in the company's interest at the close of the taxable year in which the loss occurred. All states and the District of Columbia have now passed limited liability company laws. Some states treat such companies as partnerships for tax purposes, but others treat them as corporations so state taxation must be carefully considered.

Even if an ordinary corporation has been properly formed, it may be operated in such a manner as to lose the advantages of limited liability. The phrase "piercing the corporate veil" is legal jargon referring to court action that has the effect of ignoring the existence of a corporation separate and distinct from its owners. Generally, the action involves a lawsuit by a creditor against the shareholders where the organization has been thinly capitalized (i.e., underfinanced) or where corporate shareholders have been using the corporate form as an alter ego (the legal phrase is "excessive domination").

The shareholders may be liable if it appears that the corporation was organized and operated without adequate capital to meet the obligations that could reasonably be expected to arise. The amount of capital so required is a question of fact based on the needs of the business. The shareholders may also be liable if they have treated the corporation not as a separate entity but really as a kind of alter ego of themselves, as is often the case with closely held corporations. Classically, this arises when the shareholders have failed to distinguish between the corporation's affairs and the assets of the owners (known as comingling) or when corporate procedures have not been observed (e.g., failure to hold shareholder and director meetings, and failure to keep separate books of account for the corporation, and failure actually to issue stock). Note that neither of these theories of liability requires a fraud on third parties. Of course, courts may ignore the corporate form when it has been used to evade a statutory or contractual obligation.

Although cases of piercing the corporate veil are relatively rare, owners of closely held corporations are well advised to consider the following guidelines:

1. The corporation should be adequately capitalized to meet its obligations.
2. The shareholders should not treat corporate property as if it belonged to them.
3. The separateness of the corporate form should be emphasized in the day-to-day operation of the business, so that, for example, corporate transactions are reflected on corporate rather than personal stationery, and payments are made out of corporate rather than personal accounts. No representation should be made leading others to believe that the entity is being operated on some other basis, such as a partnership (e.g., referring to a fellow shareholder as "my partner").
4. The formalities of corporate procedure (e.g., maintaining minutes of meetings) should be strictly

observed. This can have tax as well as nontax consequences. If, during the course of an audit, the agent asks to see what minutes support a bonus declared to a key shareholder, the importance of having observed such formalities will be quickly appreciated.

With respect to small businesses, if a corporation becomes insolvent, debts owed by the corporation to the shareholders may be subordinated to the claims of other creditors, so that the shareholders' claims will not be paid until all other creditors have been paid. This is the case even when a shareholder's claims have been "fully secured." Typically, such a situation arises when there has been corporate mismanagement, thin capitalization, or bad faith by the shareholder toward other creditors of the corporation. This so-called *Deep Rock* doctrine generally applies when a bankruptcy or other insolvency case is pending at a federal or state receivership proceeding. If it would be manifestly unfair to permit a controlling shareholder who has lent the company money to participate equally along with the corporation's other creditors, the court will subordinate the shareholder's loan to the claims of the company's other creditors. The procedure is sometimes referred to as equitable subordination. The revised Bankruptcy Act specifically confers upon the federal bankruptcy court the power of equitable subordination.

10

PROMOTERS

The word *promoter* does not have quite the same meaning in the law of incorporation as it does in everyday usage. In law, a promoter is understood to be one who causes a corporation to be formed, organized, and financed. The promoter(s) may be a law firm engaged for this specific purpose, the owner(s) of the proposed corporation, or someone else. (Note: An incorporator is not necessarily a promoter but is merely someone who signs the articles.)

The promoter cannot act as an agent for a corporation-to-be because that corporation does not yet exist. Thus, any contract signed by a promoter before the official existence of the corporation begins cannot be construed to be the corporation's contract or obligation. Of course, the corporation can become liable on the contract simply by adopting it. This involves the corporation's taking some affirmative act—by express words or otherwise—to adopt the contract. The adoption may also be implied from the corporation's acceptance of the benefits of the contract with full knowledge of the contract's existence.

Novation. If a promoter contracts with a third party for the benefit of a corporation to be formed, and if the corporation does not subsequently adopt the contract, the promoter will still be bound on the contract unless there is a novation. Under contract law, a novation occurs when a new contract substitutes a new party to receive benefits and to assume duties under the terms of the old contract. As an example, assume that Smith contracts to sell his home to Johnson. Before the closing date, Smith, Johnson, and Kelly execute a new agreement under which all rights and duties in connection with the transaction are transferred from Johnson to Kelly. The old Smith-Johnson contract is discharged by novation. In the context of incorporation, if a corporation adopts a preincorporation contract executed by a promoter, and if the third party agrees to accept the corporation as the debtor, there is a novation by which the corporation is substituted for the promoter.

Stock Subscriptions. There are numerous types of preincorporation agreements, including contracts for tax advice and underwriting expenses, but the classic preincorporation agreement involves the securing of subscriptions (commitments) to buy a stated number of as yet unissued shares. If the subscription is in proper written form and signed by the subscriber(s), it is irrevocable and thus enforceable by the corporation after formation. If a subscriber defaults in payment, the corporation may collect the amount owed, or, unless the agreement provides otherwise, it may rescind the agreement and sell the shares to someone else.

What is the promoter's liability if the corporation rejects the preincorporation contracts or does not do as was agreed—or never comes into existence at all? Can the other party hold the promoter liable? The answer basically comes down to whether the promoter has clearly specified that he or she is acting in the name of the proposed corporation and not individually. If so, the other party must rely on the credit standing of the proposed corporation and cannot act against the promoter individually. If not, the promoter may be held personally liable on such preincorporation contracts.

11

GETTING STARTED

As stated previously, the authority to manage the affairs of the corporation is vested in the board of directors. Provisions governing the actions of the board are set in the articles of incorporation. The board itself adopts the bylaws.

The directors set the business tone and policy and select the principal officers of the business. The directors have the right to inspect corporate books and records and properties. Generally, directors are not entitled to compensation for their services as directors unless such services are extraordinary or compensation is provided for in the articles or in a board resolution before the services are actually rendered. Note that directors are not agents of the shareholders who have elected them. Directors are fiduciaries owing their duties principally to the corporation. Their powers are derived from the state, not delegated by the stockholders.

The list of powers given to the board of directors in the RMBCA is so broad that it reduces the likelihood that an act would be found to be beyond the board's powers. In fact, even if a quorum of the company's directors cannot be assembled because of a catastrophic event, the RMBCA allows for emergency powers. In an emergency situation, the board may modify lines of succession to accommodate the incapacity of any director, officer, employee, or agent, may relocate the corporation's principal office, may designate alternative principal offices or regional offices, or may authorize the officers to do so. The board members may set the size of the board either expressly or because the number of directors is fixed in the bylaws and the board is empowered to amend the bylaws. To prevent direct manipulation of the board, however, the RMBCA provides for shareholder approval of increases or decreases in the size of the board of 30 percent or more.

In some cases, state law may permit the directors to act via conference telephone or similar communication device, without meeting face to face. Directors may also act by unanimous written consent without a meeting, unless they are restricted by the articles or bylaws. Generally, however, there is no statutory provision allowing directors to act by proxy, thus making it clear that directors are obligated to assume responsibility for making corporate decisions.

Although the authority to manage the corporation's affairs is vested in the directors as a body, often, the board will appoint committees of its own members to act for the board in certain types of matters (e.g., an audit committee). Further, many statutes authorize the creation of an executive committee, which exercises the authority of the full board subject to certain limits. For instance, the RMBCA provides that the executive committee may not authorize dividend or other distributions, fill vacancies on the board, or adopt, amend, or repeal the bylaws.

In the classic management structure, the majority shareholders elect all of the directors. If the articles include a provision for cumulative voting rights or contractual rights for the minority shareholders, then the voting procedures are somewhat different. Stockholders do not elect the president and other officers of the corporation. This is the prerogative of the board, which generally entrusts day-to-day management of the business to these officers. Minor officers may be appointed by the board or by the president. All officers serve at the pleasure of the board, although of course there may be a contract for services for a specified time period. Like any other contract, an employment contract must contain three essential elements—offer, acceptance, and consideration. If one of these elements is missing, there will be no contract. In this context, as it relates to the final element, the employee promises to perform services for the employer in exchange for the employer agreeing to pay money and other benefits. Some courts have held that a contract with an officer beyond the board's term is void. A long-term contract is more likely to be upheld if it has a duration of five years or less and if, expressly or impliedly, the directors have reserved the power to dismiss the individual for incompetence or gross abuse of position without being liable for breach of contract.

Especially in a small corporation, the same persons may serve as officers and directors and may hold more than one office, except that some state laws may prohibit the same individual from serving as both president and secretary. Persons holding more than one office should not sign corporate documents in such dual—or multiple— capacity.

Note that officers and employees are viewed as agents. This means that the corporation will generally not be bound by an agreement entered into by someone who lacked the authority to execute it. Basically, there are three kinds of authority. First, actual authority may be expressly conferred by the corporate bylaws or resolutions; in addition, an agent has implied authority to do what can be reasonably implied from a grant of express authority. Second, there is authority that the corporation allows third parties to reasonably believe the agent possesses ("apparent authority"). Third, there is authority by virtue of one's position in the corporation. This "power of position" is actually a special case of apparent authority. Even if an officer lacks *de jure* authority, if he or she exercises some authority of a corporate office, under color of title of such office, that person may be deemed a *de facto* officer.

When a vacancy on the board occurs, the remaining directors may elect a new board member. The RMBCA also gives this authority to shareholders unless the articles of incorporation provide otherwise. Note that persons exercising the functions of directors under some color of office, despite their lack of proper qualifications, election, or other requirements necessary for *de jure* directors, or despite even their removal, may still bind the corporation as *de facto* directors. Further, anyone assuming to act as a director is subject to the duties of a director.

A vacancy may occur in a number of ways. First, a director may resign at any time by delivering written notice to the board, its chair, or to the corporation itself. The resignation is effective when the notice is delivered, unless the notice specifies a later date. Second, a director may be removed by a judicial proceeding upon a finding that the director engaged in fraudulent or dishonest conduct or a gross abuse of authority or discretion. The court must find that such removal is in the best interests of the corporation. Third, the shareholders may remove the director with or without cause, unless the articles provide the directors may be removed only for cause. Where cumulative voting is authorized, special rules apply to the removal of directors. Note that some affirmative expression of assent to serve as a director is required. Thus, the courts will not impose the duties and liabilities of a director unless the individual assumes the functions of a director. A director elected to fill a vacancy must stand for election at the next annual meeting of shareholders even if the term otherwise would continue beyond the meeting. Some jurisdictions follow earlier versions of the MBCA and provide that directors elected to fill a vacancy remain in office for the term of their predecessor.

In some cases, an agreement may be entered into among the directors or between a director and a shareholder, committing the directors to vote in a particular manner. At common law, such a contract was invalid because the corporation is entitled to the unfettered discretion of the board. However, if a close corporation is involved and the agreement involves specified narrow areas such as the declaration of dividends or the selection of officers, it might be permitted. Thus, if a company has three shareholders who agree among themselves as directors that they will distribute 40 percent of the profits to the shareholders as dividends, the agreement is probably sufficiently narrow as to be acceptable.

Under the RMBCA, following the formation of a corporation, there is an organizational meeting. If the initial directors have been named in the articles of incorporation, those directors meet to appoint officers, adopt bylaws, and carry on any other business brought before the meeting. If initial directors have not been named in the articles, the incorporator(s) hold an organizational meeting to elect a board of directors.

The RMBCA makes it clear that action required to be taken by incorporators at an organizational meeting may be taken without a meeting if the action taken is supported by one or more written consents describing the action taken and is signed by each incorporator. In any case, the incorporators or the board of directors adopt the initial bylaws, which are the rules for the internal government of the corporation.

After the corporation has been organized there are two kinds of shareholder meetings—annual and special. For annual meetings the bylaws generally fix the date. Although the most important function is to elect the directors, the agenda may include reports from management, consideration of resolutions introduced on behalf of management, and such other matters as may properly come before such meetings. The notice of the meetings will usually set forth the purposes. Special meetings are held between the annual meetings and may be called pursuant to state law, the articles, or the bylaws. The business conducted at the meeting must be confined to the purposes set forth in the notice. Hence, shareholders are entitled to receive notice of, and to be represented in person or by proxy at, the meetings. A notice should not only identify the place, day, and hour of the meeting but also, in case of special meetings, the purpose for which the meeting is being called. Notice may be waived before or after a meeting and in some cases by participation of shareholders without objection to lack of notice. There has been some confusion in the law over the effect of shareholder attendance at a meeting. Generally, such attendance waives any objection to lack of notice unless the shareholder, at the beginning of the meeting, objects to holding the meeting or transacting business at the meeting. Attendance at the meeting also waives objection to the consideration of a specific matter not within the purposes described in the notice, again unless the shareholder objects to consideration of that matter when raised. When a shareholder so objects to the consideration of a matter not included in the purposes stated for the meeting, the corporation can cure that defect by receiving written waivers of notice from all the stockholders. These rules are designed to prohibit a disgruntled shareholder from raising technical objections to the outcome of a meeting at the end of the meeting rather than earlier.

In order to provide the proper notice there must be a voting list. State laws generally require a corporation to keep at its principal place of business or at the office of its transfer agent or registrar, a shareholder list, giving names and addresses of all shareholders and the number and class of shares held by each. This list is a record open to reasonable shareholder inspection. Such a list is especially important if there must be a court hearing either to compel or to enjoin the holding of a meeting.

Whether the meeting is annual or special, a quorum is required in order to start the meeting officially. (Courts are split as to whether a meeting that begins with a quorum may continue after some shareholders walk out so that less than a quorum is present.) Unless otherwise specified in the articles of incorporation, a majority of the shares entitled to vote constitutes a quorum in most states.

Voting. Shareholders generally are entitled to one vote for each share of stock they own. Most matters are decided on the basis of majority rule. Some variations may be specified in the articles of incorporation or the bylaws. The election of directors, for instance, can be decided either by straight voting—one vote per share for each directorship open, in which case the majority shareholders would elect all the directors—or by cumulative voting, so that shareholders could vote all their shares for one director, in which case there is a better chance for minority representation on the board. Other variable requirements include that for a supermajority (in which a high percentage—say, 80 percent—of the stockholders must vote in favor of an action) or a superquorum, in which more than a simple majority of the shareholders must attend in order for there to be a quorum.

A few courts and state laws have not looked favorably on such super requirements, finding them overly restrictive to the rights of the majority. For example, with a superquorum, a shareholder could deliberately remain absent, thus preventing a quorum at a meeting intended to vote on matters to which he or she was opposed. Some early court decisions did strike down such arrangements, but more recent decisions have tended to uphold them, as necessary to meet the special needs of the closely held corporation.

As has been noted, supermajority requirements may lead to deadlock, since they can allow a minority shareholder to block proposed corporate action. In cases where the election of new directors is blocked, the bylaws could provide that the directors will continue in office until their successors are elected. Other shareholder agreements provide for a dispute resolution mechanism. This allows the shareholders themselves to devise standard procedures for resolution *before* a dispute actually arises—at which time each side would otherwise press for a procedure favorable to its own interests. Further, different classes of stock can be set up to keep voting control of the corporation within a family or funding group. However, only if the share certificates contain a conspicuous notation as to their "close" status and the shareholder agreements so indicate will any transferee of shares covered by the agreement or special provision in the articles be bound.

Meeting Format. The general format of a shareholders meeting includes a secretary's report, a treasurer's report, election of directors, old business, and new business. The format of a board of directors meeting is similar, except that here the elections are for company officers. Meetings of the directors are held at least annually and sometimes more frequently, depending on the size and complexity of the business, for it is the directors who are legally responsible for the running of the corporation. They may delegate powers to the top officers, who are often themselves directors, but it is the board that holds the ultimate authority to manage the corporation's affairs.

Valid action can occur only if the directors act as a body at a validly convened meeting and not through individual deliberations. Directors vote per capita and generally may not vote by proxy. A validly convened meeting is one with the proper notice and a quorum present. A majority of those present thus has the power to decide any issues that come before the meeting.

12

PROFESSIONAL CORPORATIONS

There are a number of reasons why professionals should consider incorporation. Although the IRS now respects the existence of the incorporated professional, the battle was not an easy one. In 1954, the U.S. Court of Appeals for the Ninth Circuit held in the famous *Kintner* decision, 216 F.2d 418, that a common-law association of doctors, which ran a clinic, would be taxable as a corporation and thus could legally maintain a tax-qualified pension plan for its members. The initial response of the IRS was not to follow the *Kintner* decision, but subsequently it agreed to do so.

Under the so-called *Kintner* regulations, an association was defined as an unincorporated firm that directed a continuing enterprise for profit and that had a majority of the following corporate features: continuity of life, centralization of management, free transferability of interests, and limited liability. State law was to be followed as to whether an entity met the foregoing characteristics. Such regulations effectively make it impossible for a proprietorship or partnership to realize corporate treatment, but they left the door open for state legislatures to enact laws that permit professionals to realize the advantages of incorporation. They did so. Currently, if a professional corporation or association is valid under state law, it will be respected as such for federal tax purposes.

Generally, the professional corporation law is a supplement to the state's business corporation act, which is also applicable to professional corporations except in case of conflict where the more specific legislation will take precedence. Because professional corporation laws vary among the states, they must be studied carefully before incorporation is to be undertaken.

Under these laws, only persons licensed to practice the particular profession can own an interest in the corporation. For example, upon the death of a licensed dentist who held an interest in a professional corporation or association, the estate would have to sell his or her interest to the business itself or to another licensed dentist. Some states provide for an immediate redemption or other sale of the deceased's stock; others provide for the disposition of stock within a limited time (e.g., 90 days). Some states actually establish the price for the shares (or a formula for determining the price); others require that the articles or bylaws provide for the purchase or redemption of the shares upon the death of the shareholder. Some states provide that, absent a provision in the articles, bylaws, or an agreement, the corporation must purchase the shares owned by the deceased.

Importantly, an incorporated professional will not be personally liable for the negligent acts of any associates, as is the case with a partnership. In fact, a professional in a partnership may be liable even if he or she did not participate in the transaction out of which the liability arose. Incorporated professionals remain liable to clients or patients for their own negligence and, perhaps, for the negligence of anyone under their supervision and control. This represents a broader liability than exists in ordinary corporations but a narrower liability than would result in a professional partnership.

Other aspects of these laws generally require that shareholders in the corporation practice the same profession and, typically, even the same specialty. The minimum number of incorporators is commonly one, but some states require two (or even three). As regards the number of directors and officers required, many states allow a solo practitioner to serve as sole director and hold all of the corporate offices.

Practitioners who incorporate must comply with the usual requirements: filing the articles, paying the required fees, adopting the bylaws at the required meeting, filing the annual reports, holding stockholder and director meetings, keeping minutes, and satisfying other indicia of corporateness. Like the sole shareholder of a closely held corporation, the incorporated practitioner must treat the corporation as such, or else the corporate identity will not be respected. It is crucial that the shareholders deal with the outside world in their business and not in their personal capacities. The corporation should file all annual reports required by law, and any indebtedness incurred should be in the name of the corporation. If shareholders are required to guarantee any notes personally, it should be made clear that they are acting as guarantors and not as principals on the debt. Insurance policies should be issued (or reissued) in the name of the new corporation, taxes should be paid by the corporation, assets should be held in the corporate name, and the corporation should be billed for all purchases made.

The corporation should request an employer identification number from the IRS and refer to itself for all purposes in its corporate name followed by the appropriate designation (P.C. or P.A.). Not only should the books of the corporation be separate from the books of the individual practitioner(s), but no records should be maintained to imply that any particular clients or patients are being serviced by a given shareholder. Thus, billing of clients or patients should be done only in the name of the corporation.

As noted, a professional service corporation is a corporation that derives its income from the performance of personal services by the owner-employee. From a federal tax standpoint, the problem is that no one definition of such a corporation applies in every case—as is true of S corporations, for example. Thus, what constitutes a personal service corporation in one connection may not be relevant elsewhere. What follows is therefore an overview of some of the principal tax issues.

A qualified personal service corporation is defined as a professional corporation engaged in specific services, so long as the stock ownership requirements are met (i.e., substantially all the stock is owned by current or retired employees, or their estates, who performed the personal services). For tax years beginning after January 1, 1993, such corporations are subject to a flat tax rate of 35 percent and are thus ineligible for the graduated tax rates applicable to C corporations generally. Note that this tax applies unless the corporation files an S election. Also, whereas a C corporation must adopt the accrual basis of accounting, the qualified personal service corporation is exempt from this requirement and may elect to use the cash method of accounting. The cash basis is beneficial, since earnings are not taxed until received or deemed to be constructively received.

The stock ownership test for a qualified personal service corporation is "substantially all" of the stock. In the so-called single-customer personal service corporation, the stock ownership test is a mere 10 percent. The IRS targets such single-customer personal service corporations and is empowered to reallocate income and deductions when: (1) the principal activity of the corporation is the performance of services provided by employees owning more than 10 percent of the stock; (2) substantially all the services are performed for one corporation, partnership, or entity; and (3) the principal purpose for forming the corporation is to avoid income tax. Note that the fields of service are not limited to the usual areas (e.g., law, accounting) and that the stock attribution rules apply. These rules provide that constructive ownership exists through a related company when the shareholder owns at least 10 percent of that stock.

13

CORPORATE DUTIES

The company's board of directors is responsible for the general management of the affairs of the corporation. Significant decisions are generally entrusted to the board, although the board may delegate many matters to its corporate officers. Directors and officers alike owe fiduciary duties of care and loyalty to the corporation and to the shareholders. That is, they are required to act in the best interests of the corporation with "undivided and unselfish" loyalty and to use that degree of care in the management of the business that ordinary and prudent people would use in similar circumstances in the handling of their own affairs. Although the following description will emphasize the role of the directors, the same general principles apply to the officers, except that the scope of an officer's obligations is determined partly by the position he or she occupies.

Under the RMBCA, the duties of a director, including those duties as a member of a committee, must be discharged: (1) in good faith, (2) with the care an ordinarily prudent person in a like position would exercise under similar circumstances, and (3) in a manner that the director reasonably believes to be in the best interests of the corporation.

The RMBCA goes on to provide that a director is entitled to rely on information, opinions, reports, or statements, including financial statements and other financial data, if they are prepared or presented by:

1. One or more officers or employees of the corporation whom the director reasonably believes to be reliable and competent in the matter presented.

2. Legal counsel, public accountants, or other persons whose opinions the director reasonably believes merit confidence.
3. A committee of the board of directors (of which the director is not a member) whose deliberations the director reasonably believes merit confidence.

A director who fails to measure up to the required level of care in discharging his or her duties and thereby injures the corporation will be liable to the corporation for damages caused. In these cases the business judgment rule is commonly invoked. Under this rule, a director will not be held responsible so long as his or her acts are taken in the exercise of informed business judgment arrived at through reasonable care and reflection and a complete review of the alternatives. As an example, the acceptance of a note for a judgment, rather than enforcing it for execution, has been held to fall within the rule. However, a director will not be acting in good faith if his or her knowledge concerning a matter forestalls reliance on business judgment otherwise permitted by law. Clearly, a director may not invoke the rule if doing so causes the corporation to engage in acts that are illegal or contrary to public policy.

Some directors defend themselves for lack of diligence in corporate actions by stating that they had only served gratuitously or as figureheads. Such defenses have generally been rejected by the courts. Similarly, old age, bad health, and other disabilities have been held not to constitute good defenses, although some courts have applied these factors in reaching a decision.

Conflict of Interest. The requirement that directors act in good faith is often referred to as the duty of loyalty to serve the broad interests of the corporation. Directors thus may not serve their own interests at the expense of the corporation. The problem may arise when a director contracts with the corporation or when the corporation contracts with another entity in which one of its directors or officers is directly or indirectly involved.

At common law, a director's interest in a contract with the corporation made the contract voidable at the option of that corporation without regard to fairness. Today, in many states, a corporation's contract with an interested director will not be voidable solely because of the director's interest if the contract is fair and reasonable to the corporation or if all material facts, including the director's interest, are disclosed to the shareholders.

The RMBCA deals with the conflict-of-interest problem by providing that such a transaction will not be voidable by the corporation solely by reason of the director's interest in the transaction if any of the following is true:

1. The material facts of the transaction and the director's interest were disclosed or known to the board of directors or a committee of the board and the board or committee authorized, approved, or ratified the transaction.
2. The material facts of the transaction and the director's interest were disclosed or known to the shareholders entitled to vote and they authorized, approved, or ratified the transaction.
3. The transaction was fair to the corporation.

The conflict-of-interest problem can arise in closely held corporations. For instance, a director may obtain an interest in a business competing with the corporation, or a director may purchase a claim, debt, or obligation owed to the corporation. The duty of loyalty bars all directors from taking for themselves any advantage or business opportunity that properly belongs to the corporation; each director owes the corporation a right of first refusal, which means a right to acquire the opportunity on the same terms as were offered to the director.

Another conflict-of-interest problem can arise in regard to compensation for services rendered. Thus, a dissident minority shareholder might file suit alleging that excessive compensation was paid to a director, with resultant harm to the corporation. Although directors are not ordinarily entitled to compensation for performing the usual and customary duties of their office, the board is empowered to fix the compensation of directors unless otherwise provided. The board is also empowered to fix salaries of others for services actually rendered. The point is that any payment over and above reasonable compensation may be attacked as wasteful.

Indemnification. The fact that liability may ensue in so many different contexts means that eligibility for indemnification from the corporation can be extremely important. State statutes vary, and much depends on whether the defendant prevails in the case. Generally, if a director—or officer—is accused of wrongdoing and wins, state law will permit the corporation to reimburse the director for litigation expenses. If the defendant settles the case or loses, however, a different result may apply. This is why laws in many states permit a corporation to carry insurance to protect the corporation against liability to directors and officers for indemnification and to protect the officials involved against any liability arising out of their service to the business. Regardless of whether state law specifically authorizes the purchase of such a D&O (directors and officers) policy, the power to do so is probably implied in the corporate power to provide executive compensation.

Overall, the business judgment rule will insulate managers for mistakes of judgment arrived at in good faith. Directors and officers alike owe a fiduciary duty to act in good faith and in the best interest of the corporation. Directors may be held liable for improper dividends and distributions just as officers may be held responsible for an improper denial of access to corporate books and records. It is worth noting that officers and agents are generally liable for any acts committed, even if such actions are within the scope of their employment. Moreover, the corporation would be liable under the agency doctrine of *respondeat superior*. An officer could be held personally liable on a contract if it is shown that the officer was the "alter ego" of the corporation or if the officer signed as an individual rather than as an agent for the corporation.

14

FOREIGN BUSINESS

No matter how small or large it is, a corporation is incorporated in only one state. This is its home state, its legal domicile regardless of where its principal offices are located. For example, the Ford Motor Company (like many other large corporations) is incorporated in Delaware even though its headquarters and several of its major plants are in the state of Michigan.

Corporations that are organized under the laws of one state may operate in all or any other states. A corporation that does business in this way is referred to as a "foreign" corporation by the other state. One important fact that such foreign corporations must take into account is that they may have to qualify in order to begin "doing business" in any state other than their home state. Thus, corporations engaged in a foreign jurisdiction will be subject to that state's terms and conditions on foreign corporations before they will be permitted to engage in business in the state. This commonly entails a corporation's registering with the secretary of the state(s) where it must qualify (licensing). The tricky part is that there is no easily understood or universally accepted definition of that key phrase "doing business." The one certainty is that state laws do not define this phrase in the same way that the average businessperson would define it.

Corporations engaged in interstate commerce do not have to worry about this problem unless their business also involves substantial intrastate activities. They are protected by Article I, Sections 8 and 9 of the U.S. Constitution, which give Congress the responsibility for regulating interstate commerce and prohibit the states from interfering with such commerce. But in other instances, especially when a corporation engages in what is essentially intrastate commerce in two or more states, individual state laws apply. The question remains: What constitutes doing business within another state?

Ordinarily, maintaining a bank account in the foreign jurisdiction will not constitute doing business in the state. Neither will creating (as borrower or lender) or acquiring indebtedness, mortgages, or other security interests in real or personal property. Similarly, securing or collecting debts or enforcing any rights in property or effecting sales through independent contractors will not constitute doing business. An isolated transaction, which amounts to less than a substantial part of the business, generally won't require qualification. Even the holding of shareholders or directors meetings in the state won't constitute "doing business." Neither will the installation of equipment or the mere solicitation of stock subscriptions generally trigger licensing. On the other hand, maintaining an office or place of business within a state will be indicative (albeit not conclusive) that the foreign corporation is doing business there.

An insightful guideline is offered by an often quoted 1942 decision in Alabama: "It is established by well considered general authorities that a foreign corporation is doing, transacting, carrying on, or engaging in business within a state when it transacts some substantial part of its ordinary business therein."

If a corporation is doing "substantial" business in a state or states other than its home state, it must be in compliance with the statutes of the state(s) in question. Since most businesspeople do not have the time or the expertise to take on the task of checking the out-of-state corporate statutes, it follows that in cases where there is substantial doubt about whether qualification is necessary, the corporate officers or directors should consult qualified local legal counsel.

Failure to qualify may result in a state's fining or otherwise penalizing a foreign corporation. In extreme cases, directors or officers may be found liable for the failure to comply with local laws. For example, Oregon law subjects directors, officers, and agents to fines and/or imprisonment.

Perhaps more importantly, a corporation may not be recognized by the courts of the foreign state, and thus may find it difficult to enforce its contracts, collect its debts, and otherwise act as a full-fledged corporate citizen of the state. Note that the validity of the contracts entered into by the corporation will not be impaired. The corporation may defend an action based on a contract, but it may not be able to maintain an action until it has obtained a certificate of authority. This bar is substantive in nature and applies to a diversity action brought in federal court. As an example, under Florida law, no action, suit, or proceeding may be maintained by a foreign corporation until the corporation is authorized to do business in the state. A complaint thus filed by a nonqualified foreign corporation is subject to dismissal if the foreign corporation did not have a certificate of authority at the time the proceedings commenced—or fails to so qualify subsequently—even if the foreign corporation ceases to transact business in the state during the course of the legal proceedings. Moreover, under Florida law, a successor to an unqualified foreign corporation may not institute any proceedings in Florida arising out of the foreign corporation's business within Florida until the corporation or its successor has qualified to do business in Florida. This is intended to prevent the corporation from evading the law by simply assigning the claim to a related company. Finally, it is often less expensive to incorporate in a foreign jurisdiction than it is to qualify to do business there. If there are any doubts contact a lawyer.

15

CORPORATE FINANCE

Insofar as corporate finance is concerned, there are basically two kinds of securities: debt securities and equity securities. A debt security represents that the corporation has borrowed funds from the secured party and is obligated to repay them. An equity security is an instrument representing an investment in the business in which the shareholder becomes an owner of the corporation. The totality of the enterprise's debt and equity securities is known as the *capital structure*. Those interested in security transfer issues should be certain to consult Article 8 of the Uniform Commercial Code (UCC), which has been adopted by all states except Louisiana and governs the original issue and transfer of not only stock but also all corporate securities. For a restriction on the right to transfer shares to be valid and enforceable, the owner's consent to the restriction must be obtained and the restriction must be reasonable. Transferees of shares of corporate stock will be bound by restrictions on their right to "alienate" such shares if they take the shares *with notice* of the restriction.

Debt Securities. An important consideration for growing businesses is how to secure the cash needed both for operating and for capital expenses. Short-term loans are useful, for example, in financing receivables for short periods. If a corporation's credit standing is good, a bank may lend the funds on an unsecured basis. The bank may be willing to establish a line of credit in favor of the corporation by committing itself for a specified period to granting loans up to a fixed maximum amount.

Such a line of credit may avoid delays in consummating loans when there is an immediate need for cash.

Especially with newer ventures, however, a bank may require that the loan be guaranteed by one or more principal shareholders. This can be done without jeopardizing either the corporation's status as an independent legal entity or the limited liability of the shareholders (other than making them personally responsible for the specific debts involved). Debts can also be secured by a lien against some of the corporation's assets. Such security may be required even when the borrower has a good credit history. An assignment of accounts receivable is a form of security routinely used.

Debt financing is valuable because of the concept of leverage. Leverage (or "trading on the equity") applies when the corporation is able to earn more on the borrowed capital than the total cost of that capital. These excess earnings increase the corporation's total rate of return on the invested capital. This is particularly true with long-term borrowing, which can finance additional plant and equipment. Of course, if a corporation overexpands, borrowing too much money and not earning enough to pay off the debt, the leverage works the other way, perhaps leading to bankruptcy.

Types of Debt Securities. *Debentures* are typically unsecured obligations involving only the personal obligation of the obligor, with longer terms than other unsecured indebtedness.

Bonds are debt obligations generally understood to be backed by collateral, perhaps a mortgage against real estate or a lien on other fixed assets. Because of the presence of the security interest, the interest rate on bonds is usually lower than on debentures, and the bond maturity may be longer. Bonds are often bearer instruments, meaning that they are negotiable by delivery. The interest payments are represented by coupons that are submitted for payment. Notes are generally payable to the order of a party and the interest payments are contractual obligations not represented by a coupon. Recognize that bonds may also be registered with an issuer and transferred only by endorsement. Article 8 of the Uniform Commercial Code makes registered bonds negotiable. A debenture or bond is usually issued under an indenture or trust agreement between the corporation and the trustee. The indenture contains restrictive covenants or negative pledges and confers powers on the trustee that are intended for the protection of the holders of the obligations.

Smaller corporations tend to make extensive use of term loans. Such loans may be arranged for varied periods, although banks often will not lend for more than five years on such a basis. With a term loan, the terms and conditions are set forth in an agreement that may also contain covenants restricting the borrower in the conduct of the business. Thus, there may be a requirement that working capital be maintained at a specified minimum level. Further, the agreement may contain negative covenants under which the borrower agrees not to create or permit to exist any mortgage, lien, or other encumbrance against its business assets, except those incurred in the ordinary course of business, or not to incur capital expenditures, or not to make loans or advances to others in excess of specified amounts.

Note that debt securities are generally subject to redemption and that the securities chosen for redemption may be chosen by lot or by some other means. Debt securities can be converted into equity securities such as common stock on some predetermined basis. When the convertible debentures are converted, they—and the related debt—disappear with the new securities (called the conversion securities) issued in their place. Convertible debentures are usually redeemable. Although the RMBCA does not give debenture holders the power to vote, it should be noted that some states permit holders of bonds to participate in the election of the directors either generally or upon particular contingencies such as a default in payment.

Equity Financing, or Stock. The restrictions that often accompany debt financing may lead to a decision to avoid a loan agreement and to obtain permanent financing instead through the sale of stock. Equity securities, which give the holders a share of the corporation, generally have no fixed maturity and contain no restrictions on the conduct of the business.

Types of Stock. There are two general types of conventional equity securities—common stock and preferred stock—although certain forms of hybrid securities exist as well, combining features of debt securities and of shares. Whether hybrid securities are treated for tax purposes as debt or equity generally depends on whether there is a fixed maturity, a fixed return, and ranking with respect to general credit. Note that companies with only one class of stock are said to have only common stock as evidenced by a certificate. Recognition of the shareholder's status as such generally depends on record ownership.

The types and characteristics of stock and the implications of distributing shares in a corporation are described below. In brief, common stock is generally characterized by the fact that its rate of return is not fixed. Dividends may be increased or decreased or even omitted depending on the company's performance. Common stockholders own a share of the business and are entitled to vote their shares in the election of directors and on other matters brought before the shareholders. Holders of common stock are entitled to the net assets of the corporation, after allowance for debt and senior securities, either during the life of the corporation (under certain circumstances) or, more commonly, during liquidation. Preferred stock generally pays dividends at a fixed rate and has preference over common stock in such payments and in any distribution of the corporation's assets. Thus, preferred stock commands a fixed dividend that must be satisfied before earnings can be distributed to the common shareholders; further, the dividends on preferred stock may be cumulative so that dividends on common stock cannot be paid until all previously unpaid preferred dividends are satisfied. As will be discussed, the preferred shares may be participating or nonparticipating and have other variations.

All for-profit corporations issue shares of stock that represent ownership in the enterprise. The stock is given in exchange for money, property, or services. Thus, in setting up a corporation that will issue 1,000 shares of common stock, the incorporators may issue themselves each 400 shares in exchange for services performed; they may issue 150 shares to an investor who provides funds for them to purchase needed machinery and materials; and they may issue 50 shares to a real estate owner who deeds over to them a building in which they can set up their factory.

There are two major types of stock: common and preferred. Within these categories there are many types and classes of stock, some that can be used even by small, new corporations to accomplish various objectives, such as keeping control in the hands of the founders.

Common Stock. If a corporation has only one type of stock, it is common stock. The rate of return on common stock is not fixed; dividends are declared by the board of directors and generally depend on corporate performance. Under the RMBCA, there are two basic attributes of common stock. First, holders of common stock are entitled to vote for the election of directors and on other corporate matters. Second, holders of common stock as a group are entitled to all the net assets of the corporation (after making allowance for debt and senior securities) when distributions are made, either during the life of the corporation or during liquidation.

Under the RMBCA, these two characteristics may be divided between different classes of stock so that there may be no single class of stock that can clearly be said to be the only "common stock." Nevertheless, the RMBCA provides that at least one share of each class with either of these attributes must be outstanding. Various state laws enable corporations to create classes of common stock with distinct rights or privileges. Thus, Class A stock might be entitled to two votes per share, and Class B stock might be entitled to one vote per share. Or Class A stock might be entitled to elect more directors than Class B stock or be entitled to greater dividends.

Common stock may be either voting or nonvoting, an important distinction for purposes of establishing corporate control within a particular group. It should be noted, however, that in some states the right to vote cannot be denied a class of stock and special rules apply where organic (fundamental) changes in the corporation are contemplated.

Preferred Stock. In general, preferred stock may be voting or nonvoting and is entitled to a preference in the distribution of dividends and/or in the assets of the business upon the liquidation of the corporation. Hence, the term *preferred* refers to the right to receive payment (either as a fixed dividend or as a liquidating distribution or both) before the common shareholders receive anything. In general, preferred shares contain both preferences.

Preferred shares may also be participating or nonparticipating. Both types are entitled to a particular dividend before anything is paid out on the common shares, but only participating preferred shares are also entitled, after the common shareholders receive a stated amount, to share with them in subsequent distributions. Preferred dividends are generally cumulative; if a dividend is not paid during a year, that dividend will not be lost but will "cumulate" (i.e., it will be regarded as a corporate debt, until paid). Thus, the preferred shareholders must receive all of their accumulated dividends, as well as their current dividend, if any, before the common shareholders can receive a dividend. Moreover, if there are unpaid cumulative dividends at the time of liquidation, they must be paid first before there is any distribution of assets to the remaining shareholders.

Preferred shares may be *redeemable*—that is, the corporation may buy them back—at a stated price. Further, they may be convertible, at the option of the shareholder, into common stock, at a stated ratio or price. Generally, the price of the common shares must appreciate significantly before it becomes profitable for preferred shareholders to convert their stock. Once the shares have been converted, they are "canceled," which means that they are returned to the status of authorized but unissued shares. Ordinarily, preferred shares are nonvoting, but this must be stated in the articles of incorporation, or else the preferred shareholders might be allowed to vote in proportion to the number of preferred shares outstanding.

Authorized Shares. A corporation is empowered to issue the number of shares authorized in the articles. This is known as the corporation's authorized stock or authorized capital. Generally, there is no upper limit on the number of shares that may be authorized. Thus, a company could authorize a million shares even though it intended to issue only 100. Authorized stock is not capital stock; the latter is based on the number of shares outstanding, those actually issued. Authorizing additional shares over what is needed immediately allow for contingencies and eliminates the necessity to amend the articles later if more capital is needed. On the other hand, authorizing an excessive number of shares may cause concern to investors, who may fear that authorized shares may be subsequently issued by the board without shareholder approval. In addition, some states base their stock or franchise taxes on the number of shares authorized.

Issued Shares. The process by which all or part of the corporation's authorized stock is sold is known as the issuance of shares. Such issuance requires action by the board in accepting an offer to subscribe for shares of the corporation, and then directing the secretary to issue appropriate share certificates upon receipt of the stated consideration. Prior to incorporation, subscription agreements may be made obligating the subscribers to purchase, and the new corporation to sell, the particular shares.

Par Value. Although the RMBCA omits the principle of par value in its treatment of authorized shares, many jurisdictions still reflect this concept, which is simply an arbitrary value assigned to a share. At one time, par value represented the actual selling price of the shares, but today it is of far more limited significance. In the context of par value stock, when the value of the consideration—whether cash or some other form of payment—received is less than the par value, the stock is said to be "watered." Such stock is not deemed fully paid and nonassessable, and the shareholder may be liable for the difference between the par value and the amount paid. The classic watered-stock situation arises when a promoter transfers to the corporation overvalued property in exchange for par value stock in the corporation. Thus, par value represents a floor beneath which shares may not be issued. In the case of no-par shares, the consideration is set without regard to a minimum imposed by par value.

Stated Capital. A concept that is closely related to par and no-par value is that of minimum capital and stated capital. The trend in state laws is not to require any particular amount of minimum capital—although there clearly must be some initial capital. The level of capital actually necessary is relevant for determining whether the business was so underfunded that the corporate veil can be pierced. Technically, what is known as stated capital must be at a level that it cannot be considered to be impaired; thus, it must afford at least some protection to creditors.

What is stated capital? Under Florida law, for example, it is the sum of the par value of the outstanding par shares plus the total consideration received for all the no-par shares (excepting the portion transferred to capital surplus), plus any amounts transferred to stated capital

81

on the issuance of shares either as stock dividends or otherwise. In a no-par offering, Florida law provides that the entire consideration received constitutes the stated capital. The board may allocate to capital surplus any portion of this consideration for the issuance of shares without par value, subject to certain exceptions.

For example, assume that Jones buys all of the assets of the Darby Corporation, paying $50,000 in cash and giving a note for $150,000. Jones then decides to incorporate. (Normally he would have incorporated first.) He transfers all of the Darby assets and liabilities in a bill of sale to the new corporation, complies with any bulk transfer law, and receives the stock. Presumably, the fair value of that stock would be $50,000. Assuming a par value of $1 per share, with Jones receiving 100 shares, the total par value would be $100. The difference between that amount and the $50,000 fair value, $49,900, would be allocated to surplus. Jones has stock worth $50,000, and the corporation has $50,000 of capital and $150,000 of liabilities. The corporation also has $200,000 in assets—the amount Jones paid for the Darby assets.

Having bought a company's assets, the buyer is entitled to a "fresh start," so that he or she can depreciate the purchased assets to the extent of their value. Had Jones purchased Darby's stock instead of its assets, there would have been no such fresh start. (Among other problems connected with the purchase of stock, buyers may find that they have also acquired certain liabilities of the corporation, such as for back wages or taxes. This and other possible pitfalls can be covered in the contract of sale, but with the purchase of assets, buyers can generally see what they are getting.)

Until recently, the IRS maintained a strict distinction between tangible and intangible assets. Thus, in a purchase of assets it was generally to the buyer's advantage to allocate as much as possible to the tangible, depreciable assets and as little as possible to goodwill, which was not amortizable, whereas the seller's advantage lay in the opposite direction—in emphasizing intangibles—in order to minimize any gain (hence tax) on the sale. This was a matter to be negotiated as part of the sales agreement—but there was no guarantee that the IRS would accept the valuations specified in the agreement. The best practice was to obtain expert appraisals of the assets, so as to have an objective opinion of their value. Further, when it came to specific categories of assets, such as customer or subscriber lists, obtained pursuant to the acquisition of a business, at issue was whether such assets were truly separable from the unamortizable goodwill of the business. Generally, such assets could be depreciated if their useful lives could be ascertained with reasonable accuracy.

Today most acquired intangibles, including goodwill, may be amortized on a straight-line basis over a 15-year period. Put differently, assets that were previously not amortizable at all (like goodwill) are now amortizable over a 15-year period. (The bad news is that certain assets that were previously amortizable over shorter periods are now subject to 15-year amortization. An example is a covenant not to compete in which a seller of a business agrees not to compete with the buyer for a period of five years; while the covenant may actually end in five years, the payments related to the same must be amortized over the full 15 years.) In any event, current tax law still does not permit amortization for self-created intangibles; it is only the purchased intangibles that qualify for such treatment.

Consideration for Shares. Generally speaking, shares are issued for cash. However, other forms of consideration are possible. Many jurisdictions distinguish between eligible and ineligible consideration. Future labor, future services, and future payments (e.g., promissory notes) are ineligible unless stock is purchased by an officer, director, or employee of the corporation under a plan, agreement, or transaction, and the board reasonably expects such to benefit the corporation. In this case, the share certificates are retained by the corporation until the promissory notes are paid.

The RMBCA takes a more liberal view of eligible consideration. The RMBCA provides that authorized shares issued by the board for consideration may consist of any tangible or intangible property or benefit to the corporation, including cash, promissory notes, services performed, contracts for services to be performed, or other securities of the corporation. Since a problem may arise if the shares are issued and the services are not performed, if the future benefits are not received, or if the notes are not paid, the RMBCA provides that the corporation may escrow the shares until the services or benefits are performed or the notes paid.

Under the older MBCA, before the corporation issues the shares, the board must determine that the consideration received or to be received is adequate. The board's determination as to the adequacy of consideration is conclusive. Once the full consideration is received, the shares are paid-up and nonassessable. The RMBCA merely requires the board to find that the consideration received or to be received is adequate. The shareholder will generally not be personally liable for the acts or debts of the corporation except by virtue of his or her own acts or conduct.

Share Certificates. Under the RMBCA, shares may or may not be represented by certificates. If certificates are issued, each one must contain on its face the following information: the name of the issuer and the fact that it is organized under the laws of the state involved; the name of the person to whom the shares are issued; and the number and class of shares and the designation of the series, if any, the certificate represents. (In complex corporate organizations, classes of stock are divisible into series, which means that they may be convertible at different ratios and that they can pay dividends at different rates, offer distinct redemption rights, and provide varying rules for liquidation payments). Alternatively, under the RMBCA, the certificate may state conspicuously that the corporation will furnish the shareholder this information in writing and without charge.

Stock certificates must be signed either manually or by facsimile by two officers designated in the bylaws or by the board, and may bear the corporate seal or its facsimile. If the person who signed a share no longer holds office when the certificate is issued, the certificate is nevertheless valid.

Treasury Stock. Subject to state law, the corporation may decide to repurchase its shares. It may either cancel the shares, returning them to the category of authorized but unissued shares, or it may hold the repurchased shares as treasury stock. Thus, treasury shares are those shares that have been issued and were once outstanding but have been reacquired by the corporation and held in its treasury. Generally, there are statutory limitations on the ability of a corporation to reacquire its own shares. For example, a corporation generally may not acquire its own shares if it is insolvent or if the acquisition would render it insolvent. In this connection, it is useful to distinguish between insolvency in the "bankruptcy sense" and in the "equity sense." In the bankruptcy sense, a corporation is insolvent if its liabilities exceed its assets. In the equity sense, a corporation is insolvent if it is unable to meet its debts as they come due. Generally, a corporation may not reacquire its shares if it is insolvent—or would be rendered insolvent—in either sense.

16

S CORPORATIONS

One of the problems associated with regular (C) corporations is that they are considered taxable entities separate and apart from their owners. This is the origin of the term *double taxation*, meaning that corporate income is often taxed twice—first at the corporate rate and second at the individual rate, when dividends are distributed to shareholders. In an S corporation, on the other hand, items of income or loss pass through directly to shareholders, allowing them to avoid double taxation and to offset losses against income generated outside of the corporation. The character of individual items is maintained so that a corporate capital gain becomes an individual capital gain, tax-exempt income keeps its status at the shareholder level, and so on.

The enactment of the 1986 Tax Reform Act lowered the maximum individual rate below the maximum corporate rate, making S corporation status more attractive for businesses generating taxable income. Generally, the higher a corporation's taxable income, the more likely S corporation status would be beneficial even if part of the earnings were retained in the business. On the flip side, if business losses were expected, the S election would also be attractive, since the losses pass through to the shareholders, who are permitted to deduct their share of the loss in figuring adjusted gross income.

Thus, the Tax Reform Act of 1986 set a higher top corporate rate (34 percent) than the top individual rate (28 percent), plus it repealed the deduction for long-term capital gains and the exemption from corporate-level taxation of gains on the sale or distribution of assets in liquidation. The 1993 Tax Act reversed this approach, however, and now the top individual rate (39.6 percent) exceeds the top corporate rate (35 percent), which generally applies to income over $10 million. For corporate taxable income up to $50,000, the rate is 15 percent; between $50,000 and $75,000, the rate is 25 percent; and between $75,000 and $10 million, excepting one bracket, the rate is 34 percent. (Professional service corporations are now subject to a flat corporate tax rate of 35 percent.) The 1993 Tax Act retained the top individual rate on long-term capital gains at 28 percent, which reduces the shareholder-level double tax on stock gains. Subsequently, the capital gains rate has been reduced even further.

As an example, assume that an S corporation has taxable income of $400,000 and its sole shareholder has taxable income from other sources of $300,000. Assuming the shareholder has no itemized deductions subject to limitation, the marginal rate on the S corporation income is 39.6 percent, and the shareholder will pay $158,400 in tax. A C corporation would pay just $136,000 in tax. Note that although the S corporation shareholder pays $22,400 more in taxes on the same taxable income, the area is tricky because S corporation earnings are generally taxed once, whereas the C corporation income is taxed a second time when earnings are distributed as dividends. Thus, if a regular corporation has taxable income of $500,000 and distributes its after-tax earnings to its shareholders, the total tax paid will be $300,680. This is computed by adding the corporate-level tax of $170,000 (34 percent of $500,000) to the shareholder-level tax of $130,680 (39.6 percent of $330,000). If the corporation had elected S corporation status, the total tax due by the corporation and its shareholders would be $198,000 (39.6 percent of $500,000).

Although today's laws have made the partnership and the S corporation equal in most ways, some significant differences remain between the two forms. Thus, in the case of a tax loss, members of a firm or shareholders in a corporation can deduct such losses only to the extent of their basis (their investment) in the partnership or corporate stock. The difference is that the members of a partnership may each include their share of the partnership's liabilities, but shareholders in an S corporation may not count their share of the corporation's liabilities, in computing their basis. Thus, in such cases, S corporation shareholders get less benefit from a tax loss than do partners.

As an example, assume an S corporation is capitalized with $100,000 and that the corporation borrows $300,000 directly from a bank and the stockholder personally guarantees the loan. In this case, if the corporation loses $150,000, the shareholder can deduct only $100,000 (the shareholder's basis in the stock) on his or her personal return. If the shareholder had borrowed the money personally and lent it to the corporation, the basis would have been $400,000, and the shareholder would have been allowed to take the entire $150,000 loss as a deduction. The moral of the story is that since S corporation losses are limited to the shareholders' basis, rather than having the S corporation borrow directly from a third-party lender, the shareholders of the corporation should borrow the money personally and then lend it to the S corporation. Loans from the shareholders will thus increase their basis and allow for a greater deduction on their individual tax returns.

Another difference in the taxation of partnerships and S corporations lies in the fact that special allocations of a partnership's income may be made so long as the allocations have a substantial economic effect. An allocation has a substantial economic effect if it reflects the true economic arrangement of the partners and if it affects the dollar amount received by the partners to the same extent as the allocation. Since all shares in an S corporation must have an equal right to income, special allocations are not permissible.

Professional corporations should generally opt for the regular corporate form, since all of the net income of the business is generally payable to the professional in the form of salary except for that portion the professional finds it more profitable to retain in the corporation. Moreover, an important reason for incorporating a professional's business is to obtain a business deduction for amounts paid for fringe benefits such as group life insurance. In an S corporation, such deductions are not ordinarily available for anyone who owns more than 2 percent of the shares in the corporation.

There are various technical distinctions between C and S corporations. As an example, loans from a qualified employee plan to plan participants are legal in a C corporation but are prohibited in an S corporation. Also, an S corporation may have no more than 75 shareholders, all of whom must be "natural persons," estates, or certain trusts such as the voting trust and the so-called Subchapter S trust. Shareholders may not be nonresident aliens. Note that only residence in the United States qualifies an alien; residence in a possession or a territory will not suffice. Each individual who owns stock in an S corporation as a tenant in common, joint tenant, or tenant by the entirety is ordinarily considered a separate shareholder, but a husband and wife (and their estates) will be treated as a single shareholder.

Only domestic corporations (those organized in the United States) may elect S corporation status. Further, certain specialized entities, such as insurers that are entitled to special tax benefits not available to individuals, are ineligible to become S corporations. However, banks not using the reserve method for bad debt accounting may now elect S corporation status. Until recently, a corporation could not elect S corporation status if it belonged to a group in which one or more corporations were connected through stock ownership with a common parent corporation. However, the Small Business Act of 1996 repealed the affiliated group disqualification rules so that an S corporation is now allowed to be a member of an affiliated group. This means that an S corporation may now own 80 percent or more of a regular

(C) corporation. However, the S corporation is not permitted to file a consolidated return with affiliated C corporations, although the C corporation can still file a consolidated return with the other affiliated corporations. Note that when an S corporation owns 80 percent or more of a C corporation subsidiary, the dividends from the C corporation are not included in the S corporation's passive investment income. This exclusion will apply, however, only to the extent that the dividends are attributable to the earnings and profits from an active trade or business of the C corporation.

Interestingly, the 1996 Act allows tax-exempt organizations to be S corporation shareholders, so that charitable and educational organizations may now own S corporation stock. Also, the 1996 Act created the electing small business trust, allowing distributions to be made among a number of beneficiaries. Each beneficiary is counted toward the 75 allowable shareholders, but since no item of income or loss is allocated to a beneficiary, the tax burden is borne by the trust at the highest individual tax rates. Note that the tax liability of the trust with regard to its income—other than from the S corporation—is computed by disregarding the S corporation items. A distribution deduction is allowed, but it is figured without regard to any S corporation items.

An S corporation may have only one class of stock, so that dividend rights and liquidation preferences are equal for all shares. The stock may have differences in voting rights and still be considered a single class of stock if all other rights are identical. Nor will straight debt be regarded as a second class of stock. ("Straight debt" is a safe harbor device defined as any written, unconditional promise to pay a certain sum of money on demand or on a specified date so long as the interest rate and interest payment dates of the debt instrument are not contingent on the S corporation's profits, the borrower's discretion, or similar factors.) Further, the debt instrument cannot be converted directly or indirectly into stock, and the creditor must be eligible to own S corporation stock. If the debt does not so qualify, an inadvertent termination of S corporation status may result.

The actual election to become an S corporation is made by filing IRS Form 2553. All shareholders must consent to the election, either on the form or on separate declarations. (If any stock is held by a trust, the consent must be made and signed by the persons deemed to be the owners of the stock.) The election may be made on any date until the fifteenth day of the third month of the taxable year in which it is to be effective. A new corporation should file before the fifteenth day of the third month after the first date on which the corporation has shareholders, acquires assets, or begins business. Because filing is so critical—a request postmarked even a day late will be considered untimely—Form 2553 should be hand-delivered to an IRS office or sent via U.S. certified mail, with return receipt requested. A self-addressed, stamped envelope should be enclosed, with a request that the IRS return a copy of the filed Form 2553 to the sender. Caveat: If an S corporation election is filed after the proper due date, the S election will still be valid, but for the following tax year rather than the current year. However, the Small Business Act of 1996 allows the IRS to treat such a late-filed election as though it were filed on time if there is reasonable cause to justify the late filing. In such a case, the election will be effective for the current year.

The taxable year of an S corporation must be either the calendar year or another accounting period for which the corporation establishes a satisfactory business purpose. The reason for using a fiscal year is that shareholder income can be deferred into a later period. For example, if an S corporation has a tax year ending on August 31, the corporation's net income from September 1 to December 31 will not be taxed to the shareholder until the following year, assuming that the shareholder has a calendar year end. Moreover, when an

S corporation's fiscal year ends before the shareholder's tax year, the corporation's net income to the shareholder is a factor for tax-planning purposes. Thus, an S corporation may adopt a fiscal year if 25 percent or more of the corporation's gross receipts for the 12-month period is recognized in the last two months of the period; this requirement needs to be met for three consecutive 12-month periods. This is known as the natural business year test. The other way to qualify under the expedited procedures is via the ownership tax year test. Simply put, an S corporation may meet the ownership tax year test if shareholders owning more than half of the stock have, or adopt, the same tax year. Whenever a corporation cannot meet the natural business year or ownership tax year tests, the company may still establish a business purpose on the basis of its facts and circumstances and seek IRS approval. The IRS will look to compelling non-tax factors, however, and will charge the company a $200 fee for a business purpose application.

Section 1244 permits ordinary loss treatment, subject to limitations, for losses on the sale or worthlessness of corporate stock. Since the amount of loss is the difference between the shareholder's basis in the stock and the amount received for the stock, shareholders of regular corporations who own Section 1244 stock should consider the implications of an S election on their basis in such stock. Any losses and deductions of an S corporation, including capital losses, pass through to the shareholders and reduce their basis in the S corporation stock. Thus, any loss on the sale of Section 1244 stock will be reduced by the amount of pass-through losses. It should be noted that losses and deductions of an S corporation are passed through and recognized by the shareholders at the close of the corporate tax year in which they are incurred, whereas a loss on Section 1244 stock is recognized only when the stock is sold or exchanged.

Every S corporation must file a return on Form 1120S each tax year, even though it may not be subject to tax.

The corporation must report gross income and allowable deductions, as well as information concerning the shareholders, their holdings, and any distributions made on their pro rata shares of corporate items. If the return is based on a calendar year, it must be filed by March 15 following the close of the tax year. If an S corporation is permitted to use a fiscal year as its tax year, the return must be filed by the fifteenth day of the third month following the close of the fiscal year.

Note that although an S corporation is generally free of tax at the corporate level, the corporation may be subject to tax if it has corporate earnings and profits left over from years in which it was a regular (C) corporation at the close of a tax year and more than 25 percent of its gross receipts for the year is passive investment income (e.g., receipts from interest, dividends, rents, royalties, annuities, and gains from sales or exchanges of stock or securities). Further, when a C corporation converts to an S corporation, the preconversion appreciation it has on its assets—known as built-in gain—will be taxed to the corporation if the assets are sold or distributed within 10 years of the date that the S election became effective. Gains and losses from the capital assets generally pass through to the stockholders as capital gains and losses, but former C corporations not subject to the tax on built-in gains, because they elected S corporation status prior to January 1, 1987, may still be subject to a corporate-level tax on capital gains. Note that each shareholder takes into account his or her pro rata share of items of income, losses, deductions, or credits that the corporation has treated separately. The shareholder also takes into account his or her pro rata share of the corporation's nonseparately computed income or loss, and the S corporation's items of preference income are subject to the alternative minimum tax. In each case, the shareholder's share depends on the percentage of stock owned on each day of the corporation's tax year.

Regarding net operating losses, any such loss sustained

by an S corporation will be passed through and deducted by the shareholder—as an ordinary loss fully deductible in computing the shareholder's adjusted gross income. This loss can be carried back three years and forward 15 years. The corporation will not be permitted to deduct a carryback or carryforward loss arising in a year in which it was taxable as a C corporation, except to the extent that the income was attributable to built-in gain incurred while it was a C corporation. Although S corporation income will generally be exempt from tax at the federal level, not all states exempt such corporations from tax. Some states even require a separate election at the state level. Finally, because, under the new law, the top corporate rate is lower than the top individual rate, and the alternative minimum tax rate for C corporations can be lower than the applicable rate for S corporation shareholders, termination of the S corporation election might be considered. Although an S election is generally effective for all subsequent tax years, the election will terminate if it violates any of the eligibility requirements referred to herein or if the corporation has regular earnings and profits and more than 25 percent of its gross receipts are from passive investment income for three consecutive years.

Regarding the latter, Congress was concerned that certain taxpayers would misuse the S election rules and manipulate the S corporation to shelter certain types of passive type income from the double taxation of C corporation dividends. Thus, Congress enacted a tax on excess passive investment income that applies at the S corporation level, and the receipt of excessive amounts of passive income for three consecutive years is deemed a terminating event, disqualifying S corporation status. Note that when the corporation fails the passive income test, S status will terminate after the end of the third consecutive year. As an example, assume a company has passive investment income with greater than 25 percent of its gross receipts for 1999, 2000, and 2001. S corporation status for the company will terminate for tax year 2002.

Under the 1996 Act, however, the IRS is empowered to waive an inadvertent S corporation termination. Specifically, the corporation may continue to be treated as a valid S corporation if the IRS deems that the termination was due to inadvertent circumstances, if it takes steps to qualify as an S corporation within a reasonable period of time after discovering these circumstances, and if, during the time period involved, both the corporation and the shareholders agree to IRS adjustments consistent with S corporation tax treatment. In any event, shareholders who hold more than half of the issued and outstanding shares can revoke the election. Once the termination occurs, the corporation will not generally be able to elect S status again for five years.

It should be noted that the general tax rules under Subchapter C for regular (C) corporations, applicable to contributions, distributions, and liquidations, also apply to S corporations unless the law provides otherwise or the Subchapter (C) rules conflict with the Subchapter S rules. The 1996 Act repealed the rule that an S corporation is treated as an individual shareholder in another corporation. Thus, an S corporation can now liquidate a subsidiary in a tax-free liquidation, and when it acquires stock in another company it will be eligible to make a Section 338 election. With a Section 338 tax election, the target company receives a stepped-up tax basis for its assets because it was deemed to have made a taxable sale of those assets. The waiting period begins with the tax year when the termination becomes effective and ends with the fifth tax year thereafter, although the IRS may agree to waive the five-year waiting period if it concludes that the termination was inadvertent, if the terminating condition was beyond the control of the corporation and was cured within a reasonable period of time after the terminating event, and if the corporation and shareholders agree to make the adjustments mandated by the IRS.

It is evident that if an S corporation terminates midway through a tax year, the year will be divided into two short years—an S corporation short year and a regular (C) corporation short year, although the two short years are combined and treated as one for carrybacks and carryforwards of tax items. Both the S corporation short-year return and the C corporation short-year return will be due on the same date. If there is a sale or exchange of 50 percent or more of the stock of the S corporation during the termination year, the taxpayers must allocate between the S and the C short years by implementing an interim closing of the books. In any event, remember that an S election requires unanimity, but revocation requires a simple majority. Once S corporate status is revoked, the owners of the business may live to regret that decision, so care is warranted.

When an S corporation conveys assets, the shareholders of the corporation receive a pass-through of the gain equal to the increase in the basis in the stock. When the sales proceeds are actually distributed to the shareholders, the shareholders determine their gain or loss by comparing the value of the property received in the distribution to the adjusted basis in the stock; the basis increase allows the shareholders to receive tax-free distributions equal to the increase in basis. A stock sale has similar results, since the shareholders recognize gain by comparing the value of the cash received for the stock to the adjusted basis of the shares.

As noted previously, with the repeal of the *General Utilities* rule, regular (C) corporations are now required to recognize gain or loss on the distribution of their property in complete liquidation as if the property had been sold to the distributee at its fair market value. However, the rules are different in the liquidation of an S corporation.

Prior to the passage of the Tax Reform Act of 1986, gain on appreciated property distributed by an S corporation in complete liquidation was not recognized at the corporate level; the shareholder recognized any gain by the fair market value of the assets received minus the tax basis in the shareholder's stock.

Under the provisions of the Tax Reform Act of 1986, if an S corporation makes a distribution of property with respect to its stock and the fair market value of the property exceeds the S corporation's basis in such assets, then gain is recognized by the S corporation as if it had sold the assets at their fair market value. Further, under new Section 1374, an S corporation is required to recognize corporate-level gain over a 10-year period, beginning with the first day of the first year for which the corporation is under S corporation status.

The reason for new Section 1374 is simple. Since the 1986 Act provides for corporate recognition of gain on sales or distributions of property in the course of liquidation of a regular (C) corporation, such a company need only convert to S corporation status to avoid tax on the gain. The fact that under the Tax Reform Act of 1986 S corporations are required to recognize gain at the corporate level is not a disincentive to conversion, since the amount of the recognized gain increases the shareholder's basis for the stock, thereby decreasing the shareholder's gain on liquidation (i.e., there is still just a single tax, compared with the double taxation levied on C corporations). Congress thus provided that new Section 1374 would apply when a regular (C) corporation had converted to S corporation status if the election took place after 1986 and the corporation subject to tax had a recognized built-in gain during the 10-year period following the first day of its first S corporation year.

The tax is imposed at the highest corporate rate and applies to the lesser of the recognized built-in gain for the year or the amount that would be the taxable income of the corporation if it had been a C corporation for the year.

To find the recognized built-in gain subject to tax, you take the lowest of the following: (1) the entire recognized gain; (2) the amount of the built-in gain on the first S corporation day with respect to the property sold;

or (3) the net unrealized built-in gain on the first S corporation day minus the recognized built-in gains in prior years during the 10-year period. (The tax is applicable to the proceeds of any "disposition" of assets made during such period. Disposition means any sale or distribution, whether or not in the course of liquidation, as well as the collection of accounts receivable and the completion of contracts under the completed contract method.)

For example, assume that a regular (C) corporation elects S corporation status on February 2, 2000. Under federal tax law, if any S corporation is to be effective for a corporation's existing tax year, Form 2553 must be filed no later than the fifteenth day of the third month of the corporation's taxation year. In the case of an existing C corporation (as here) wishing to convert to S corporation status, an election must be made by March 15 to be effective for the current year; an election made after that date would be effective beginning with the following tax year.

In this case, the corporation made a timely election. Its first day as an S corporation is January 1, 2000, at which time, for the sake of simplicity, assume that it held just two assets: one with a tax basis of $20,000 and a fair market value of $60,000, the other with a tax basis of $20,000 and a fair market value of $10,000. The corporation's total basis in the assets therefore is $40,000, while the total fair market value of the assets is $70,000. This means that the net built-in gain for the assets on the corporation's first day as an S corporation is $30,000.

Now, assume that in 2000, the first asset is sold for $70,000. The built-in gain recognized for federal tax purposes is the lowest of three numbers: (1) the recognized gain, here, $70,000 minus $20,000, or $50,000; (2) the built-in gain at January 1, 2000, here, $60,000 fair market value minus $20,000 tax basis, or $40,000; or (3) the net unrealized built-in gain on January 1, 2000, less the recognized built-in gains in prior S corporation years during the 10-year period, here, $60,000 minus $0, or $60,000. The lowest of the three is $40,000, which is the amount of gain that must be recognized in 2000 for federal tax purposes. Assuming an applicable tax rate of 34 percent, the tax to the corporation will be $13,600. This means that of the total recognized capital gain of $50,000, the corporation must pay tax on just $40,000, allowing more gain to pass through to the shareholder. In this case, the pass-through is $50,000 minus $13,600, or $36,400, on which the shareholder pays individual tax. The shareholder's basis for the stock in the corporation is increased by $36,400, the amount of the pass-through.

Since the taxpayer must be able to show the original built-in gain on the first day that the corporation became an S corporation on an asset-by-asset basis, an appraisal must be made. In fact, without proof of the original built-in gain, the entire gain is treated as recognized built-in gain.

In sum, an S corporation, unlike a C corporation, is generally not subject to tax at the corporate level, although shareholders are subject to tax on the pass-through. However, there are exceptions to this rule. The one discussed here concerns the so-called built-in gains tax, designed to prevent eligible (C) corporations from converting to S corporation status in order to avoid the tax effects of the repeal of the *General Utilities* doctrine. Specifically, a corporate-level built-in gains tax is imposed on any gain that arose prior to the C conversion and that is recognized by the S corporation within 10 years after the effective date of the S corporation election. For this purpose, a built-in gain is the excess of an asset's fair market value on the date that the election became effective over the corporation's adjusted basis in the asset on such date. This law applies only to tax years beginning after December 31, 1986, and only to C corporations that make their S corporation elections after December 31, 1986; it does not apply to newly formed corporations that elect S corporation status. A different Section 1374, now known as old Section 1374, imposed a corporate-level capital gains tax if certain conditions were met. This statute does not apply if a corporation is subject to new Section 1374.

Since S corporations are now subject to a corporate-level tax on built-in gains, those contemplating the eventual sale of a business may wish to minimize the tax effect of future appreciation of such assets by making an immediate S corporation election to cap the gains that must be recognized, taking care to have appraisals taken as of the first day of the S corporation year.

The sale of corporate assets generally does not result in double taxation. If the S corporation sells assets at a gain in a transaction to which the Section 1374 built-in gains rules do not apply, the shareholders receive a pass-through of the gains, and their basis in the stock of the S corporation is increased by that amount. If the S corporation distributes property with respect to its stock and the property's fair market value exceeds its adjusted basis in the hands of the corporation—the property having appreciated—the S corporation must recognize gain as if it had sold the property at fair market value. However, unless the built-in gains rules apply, there is no double taxation, since the gain passes through to the stockholders and increases their stock basis.

17

DIVIDENDS: AN OVERVIEW

A dividend is any distribution of cash or property paid to shareholders on account of share ownership. Generally, dividends represent the portion of the corporation's profits that does not have to be retained in the treasury to finance expansion or for some other business purpose. It is up to the board of directors to decide when to declare dividends and in what form. Tax considerations are an important factor in such decisions, though less so in S corporations.

Distributions may be made in the company's own stock rather than in cash or property. A stock dividend (or share dividend) simply distributes additional shares among the shareholders. Since no cash or property is distributed, it does not reduce the true worth of the corporation or increase the true worth of the shareholder. It simply increases the number of shares outstanding without reducing assets. A stock dividend does affect stated capital (also called stated value), however. A stock dividend should be distinguished from a stock split, which divides the number of shares into a greater number and reduces proportionately the par value of the shares without affecting stated capital. Thus, no transfer from surplus to stated capital is required. (Note: Because the RMBCA has eliminated the concept of par value, no distinction is made there between share dividends and stock splits.)

Once a dividend has been legally declared, the shareholder becomes a creditor of the corporation in the amount of the dividend. To determine which shareholders are entitled to a dividend, the board may set a "record date," unless the bylaws provide a method for fixing the date. All shareholders of record as of that date are entitled to payment. The "payment date" is the day that payment is made, and the "date of declaration" refers to the day that the board passes the appropriate resolution. Some state laws regulate the fixing of the record date. If the directors do not fix a record date at all, the dividend will belong to the owners of record as of the date of declaration, regardless of who owns the stock when the dividend is paid.

In most cases shareholders have no absolute right to the payment of dividends. The board alone is empowered to determine, in its best judgment, if and when dividends should be declared and in what amounts. That is, courts will not second-guess the business judgment of directors if it is exercised in good faith or is based on the best available information. However, a shareholder may attempt to show that the board's refusal to declare a dividend was in bad faith or so unreasonable as to constitute an abuse of discretion. This circumstance can arise especially in closely held corporations, where majority interests may attempt to oppress minority shareholders by refusing to declare dividends notwithstanding the existence of large surpluses. Under North Carolina law, the directors of a closely held corporation are required to justify their refusal to pay less than one-third of the net annual profits in dividends where holders of 20 percent or more of the shares object to the board's dividend policy. Relatedly, although preferred shareholders have no guaranteed right to dividends, the articles may give them this right if corporate earnings are sufficient for payment.

There are also restrictions as to what funds should be available for distribution. Generally, cash or property dividends are payable only out of surplus (i.e., an excess of net assets over stated capital). In some states, dividends cannot be paid out of stated capital. The reason for this restriction is that the corporation's stated capital signifies amounts contributed by the shareholders to allow the corporation to operate. Creditors are permitted to rely on such amounts for payment of debts incurred by the business. Thus, directors are liable to the corporation for their declaration of unauthorized dividends.

If the capital account is impaired, whether through operating losses or some other cause, the corporation cannot declare a dividend even though it has current net profits. On the other hand, some states do allow payment of dividends out of current net profits, notwithstanding impairment of the capital account. Further, in California, a corporation may pay cash or property dividends so long as its total assets after the payment are at least equal to 1.25 times its liabilities and its current assets are at least equal to its current liabilities. Of course, no dividend may be paid contrary to any restrictions in the articles.

The MBCA provides that cash or property dividends may be declared so long as total assets are at least equal to total liabilities. For this purpose, the value of corporate assets may be based upon any fair value that is reasonable under the circumstances. There are also technical requirements related to payment of dividends out of various kinds of surplus (e.g., earned surplus, paid-in surplus). In any event, dividends are generally prohibited when the corporation is in fact insolvent or where payment of the dividend would render the corporation insolvent. Note that generally a repurchase or redemption will have the same effect as a dividend, so similar limitations apply. All these actions represent a distribution of money to shareholders without any direct benefit to the corporation.

Practical considerations relate to the declaration of dividends as well. For example, bank loan documents should be carefully examined, because there may be covenants restricting the corporation's ability to pay a dividend. Relatedly, the payment of dividends reduces equity in the business, thereby impairing the corporation's debt-equity ratio, and is thus often closely watched by creditors.

18

DIVIDENDS OF CASH OR PROPERTY

Corporate distributions of cash or property to shareholders are treated as ordinary income to the extent that the corporation has accumulated earnings and profits. In terms of the source of the distribution, a dividend is deemed initially to have been made from current earnings and profis.

The actual tax treatment depends not only on earnings and profits but also on the recipient shareholder's basis in the shares as follows:

1. The distribution is an ordinary dividend only to the extent of current earnings and profits.
2. If there are no current (i.e., this year's) earnings and profits, but there are accumulated earnings and profits from prior years, the distribution is taxable as an ordinary dividend to the extent of accumulated earnings and profits.
3. If there are neither current nor accumulated earnings and profits, the distribution is a nontaxable return of capital, with the recipient shareholders reducing their basis in the assets to the extent of the distribution.
4. If there are neither current nor accumulated earnings and profits, and the shareholder's basis in the shares is reduced to zero, the excess is taxed as a gain on the sale of the shares (ordinarily, at capital gains rates).

In sum, the corporation must maintain two accounts for earnings and profits—one for the current year and one for all previous years. If either account shows a positive balance, the distribution is taxable as a dividend. If a distribution exceeds earnings and profits, however, such excess is not taxable as a dividend but is, as explained above, a reduction in basis. Once the basis is reduced to zero, the distribution is generally taxable as a capital gain. Calculating earnings and profits is a complex exercise, but the final amount roughly corresponds to the earned surplus account, representing the retained profits from operations as well as various nonoperating items such as the sale of assets.

For example, a corporation makes a cash distribution of $150,000 to a shareholder, has current earnings and profits of $40,000, and has accumulated earnings and profits from prior years of $60,000. The tax basis for the shareholder's stock is $20,000. The tax treatment to the shareholder is as follows: (1) taxable dividend—from current earnings and profits—$40,000; (2) taxable dividend—from prior earnings and profits—$60,000; (3) nontaxable recovery of capital contribution—$20,000; and (4) taxable capital gain—$30,000. Note that earnings and profits are computed in two separate layers. The first consists of prior accumulated earnings and profits as of the beginning of the year, and the second consists of earnings and profits accumulated in the current year. Earnings and profits for each year are computed at the end of the year without deduction for current distributions—distributions are always taken from the current year's layer first with any excess taken from the prior layer of earnings. Once the layers of earnings and profits have been defined, each layer is considered to determine the taxability of distributions. Thus, a corporation can have a deficit in current year earnings and profits but can still distribute taxable dividends if the company has accumulated earnings and profits from prior years. Assume, for example, that a company has $100,000 of accumulated earnings and profits at the beginning of the year and that the company operates at a loss during the year. The company then distributes $50,000, which is taxable as an ordinary dividend, from the previously accumulated earnings and profits.

So much for cash dividends. Insofar as any property dividends—or dividends in kind—are concerned, a distribution of property to a noncorporate shareholder is measured by the fair market value of the property on the date of the distribution. The shareholder's basis in the property received is also the fair market value on the date of distribution. As is the case with cash dividends, the portion of the distribution covered by existing earnings and profits is treated as a dividend, with the excess considered a return of capital. If the fair market value of the property distributed exceeds the corporation's earnings and profits and the shareholder's basis in the stock, a capital gain results. The amount distributed is reduced by any liabilities to which the distributed property is subject immediately before and immediately after the distribution and by any liabilities of the corporation assumed by the shareholder in connection with the distribution.

Note that distributions of appreciated property may cause gain to the distributing corporation—as if the corporation had sold the property to its shareholders at a fair market value *higher than* the corporation's basis in the property. However, no loss is recognized to the distributing corporation on distributions of property with a tax basis in excess of the property's fair market value. If the distributed property is subject to a liability in excess of basis, or if the shareholder assumed such a liability, the fair market value of the property for purposes of determining gain (or loss) on the distribution is considered as being not less than the amount of the liability.

Overall, in the event of a property distribution, the earnings and profits account is reduced by the amount of cash distributed or by the greater of either the fair market value or the adjusted basis of the property distributed, less the amount of any liability on the property. Earnings and profits are increased by any gain recognized on appreciated property distributed as a property dividend. Note that such distributions cannot trigger a deficit in earnings and profits; such a deficit can only result through the generation of business losses.

For example, a company make a property distribution to a shareholder with a fair market value of $100,000 and subject to a mortgage of $50,000. The amount distributed is $100,000 − $50,000 = $50,000. Thus, the amount received is determined by fair market value less the value of any liabilities assumed by the shareholder or liabilities to which the transferred property is subject. The shareholder then receives a tax basis in the property equal to its fair market value on the date of distribution. The corporation in turn recognizes taxable gain if appreciated property other than cash is distributed, with the gain measured by the excess of the property's value over its tax basis. (In other words, the distribution is treated as though it were sold at its fair market value to the shareholder. If the property is transferred subject to a liability, the fair market value of the property will not be less than the liability.) Thus, in the above example, the mortgage of $50,000 constitutes liabilities relieved, with the taxable gain measured by the difference between the liabilities relieved and the property's adjusted tax basis.

Another type of dividend is the so-called disguised or constructive dividend. Such dividends are not declared per se but result from a corporate action such as the payment of excessive salaries or distributions for the personal benefit of shareholders. Such payments are tantamount to dividends and are so treated by the IRS. Constructive dividends reduce the earnings and profits of the corporation but are not deductible for tax purposes. They have the same tax attributes as actual distributions. One must be careful in interpreting whether a payment qualifies as a disguised dividend. For example, if a corporation pays the premiums on key person life insurance policies owned by shareholder-employees, an economic benefit has been conferred on these employees amounting to a constructive dividend. A different result would be reached, however, if the corporation were deemed to own the policies. The central point, therefore, is whether or not a measurable economic benefit has been conferred on the *shareholder* so that constructive dividend treatment results. Another example of an economic benefit conferred upon a shareholder arises when the shareholder borrows funds from the corporation with no bona fide intent to repay the same or when the corporation sells assets to a controlling shareholder at a price beneath its fair market value. Similarly, when a controlling shareholder causes the corporation to make corporate property available to his or her family rent-free, or when the corporation makes payments that benefit the shareholder directly rather than the corporation, a disguised dividend results. Thus, if the corporation pays the wages of the controlling shareholder's housekeeper, that constitutes a dividend. Less obvious, though, are cases in which the corporation pays too much in a sale of assets by the shareholder to the corporation. In this case, the sale to the corporation at an excessive price would constitute a dividend to the shareholder.

There are many instances in which a corporation may have surplus profits but little or no cash available to pay dividends because the profits have been invested in additional inventory or fixed assets. The shareholders nevertheless may desire a distribution that will not affect the financial condition of the corporation, and for this purpose the directors may pay a dividend in its own stock.

Assume, for example, that a corporation with $10,000 of capital stock and $5,000 of earned surplus can legally declare a dividend of 50 percent. Thus, it could increase its authorized capital stock to $15,000 and transfer $5,000 from the earned surplus to the capital stock account. Stock will be issued to the shareholders at the rate of one share for every two shares held. Theoretically, the status of the shareholders and their individual interests in the corporation has not changed. Thus, a shareholder who owned 10 percent of the business prior to the dividend continues to own 10 percent of the business. The assets have not been increased or decreased in this balance-sheet transaction. Only the liabilities have changed, in that an item of surplus has been transformed into a liability. In other words, before the declaration of the dividend, a holder of $1,000 in stock had 100 shares, theoretically worth $15 per share. Following the declaration of the stock dividend, the same shareholder holds 150 shares, theoretically worth $10 per share.

An understanding of the tax treatment of stock dividends and stock rights is pivotal for understanding the tax treatment of related matters such as stock redemptions. In general, stock dividends are not taxable if they are pro rata distributions of stock on common stock. Thus, in the foregoing example, the corporation has not reduced its assets or its earnings and profits, and the shareholder has not increased his or her ownership interest. Note, though, that if the shareholder receives a nontaxable stock dividend, the basis in the old stock must be allocated between the old and the new stock. The shareholder's basis is allocated in proportion to the relative fair market values of the old and new stock (i.e., the shareholder will not receive a step-up in basis, because the transfer is nontaxable).

As an example, assume that a shareholder owns 100 shares of common stock with a tax basis of $1,000 and then receives a stock dividend of an additional 100 shares of common stock in a nontaxable transaction. The market value of the new stock is the same as that of the old stock so that the tax basis of $1,000 is allocated to 200 shares; thus, all shares are assigned a tax basis of $5. If, instead, the shareholder receives a dividend of 50 shares of preferred stock, on the date of distribution the fair market value of the common stock is only $900 and the market value of the preferred stock, $100. In this case, the shareholder's tax basis in the common stock is reduced to $900 ($1,000 × 90%), and the basis in the preferred stock is $100 ($1,000 × 10%).

There are five exceptions to this general rule, however:

1. Distributions payable either in stock or in property. If any stockholder is given the choice of accepting cash or property other than stock, all stockholders will be taxed on the stock dividend; however, this exception does not apply to certain dividend reinvestment plans or to cash distributed in lieu of fractional shares. (In such cases, the cash is generally not included in the stockholder's gross income.)

2. Distributions resulting in the receipt of property by some shareholders and an increase in the proportionate interest of other shareholders in the assets or earnings and profits of the distributing corporation. Distributions of stock and cash or property are considered disproportionate only if a stock dividend on the common stock is balanced by a cash or property distribution on preferred stock or debentures that are convertible into common stock—that is, if the distribution increases the proportionate interests of at least some class of the common shares.

3. Distributions that result in the receipt of preferred stock by some common stock shareholders and the receipt of common stock by other shareholders.

4. Distributions on preferred stock—whether actual or constructive, and whether or not the distribution has a disproportionate effect—other than an increase in the conversion ratio of convertible preferred stock made solely to take account of a stock dividend or stock split with respect to stock into which the preferred is convertible.

5. Distributions of convertible preferred stock, unless it can be proved that the distribution will not result in a disproportionate distribution. The IRS generally considers such a disproportionate distribution to result when the conversion right must be exercised

shortly after the date of the stock distribution and when the dividend rates, the redemption provisions, the marketability of the convertible stock, and the conversion price indicate that some shareholders will exercise their rights while others will not.

The rules governing the tax treatment of rights to purchase stock are basically the same as the rules for stock dividends. If the stock rights are taxable, the recipient has income to the extent of the fair market value of the rights. This fair market value then becomes the recipient's basis in the rights. If the rights are exercised and the recipient buys stock, the holding period for this stock is based on the date that the rights—whether taxable or nontaxable—are exercised. The basis of the new stock is the basis of the rights plus the amount of any other consideration given up.

If the stock rights are not taxable at issuance and their value is less than 15 percent of the value of the existing stock, the basis of the rights is zero unless the shareholder elects to have some of the basis in the old stock allocated to the rights. If the fair market value of the rights is 15 percent or more of the value of the existing stock and the rights are exercised or sold, the shareholder must allocate the basis in the old stock between the stock itself and the rights in proportion to their relative market values on the distribution date. The purpose of this 15 percent demarcation is to avoid the necessity for having minimal basis adjustments on a distribution of rights of relatively small value. For example, a shareholder has 2,000 shares of common stock with a tax basis of $10,000, and receives stock rights with a market value of $4,000 in a nontaxable distribution when the stock is valued at $16,000. The shareholder must allocate his or her tax basis—the basis of the common stock is $8,000 ($10,000 × 80%), and the basis for the stock rights is $2,000 ($10,000 × 20%). Had the stock rights been valued at less than $2,400 ($16,000 × 15%), the basis for the stock rights would be zero, unless the shareholder opted to allocate basis. Should the shareholder elect to allocate basis, the election needs to be made on the tax return for the year in which the rights were received and, once made, is deemed irrevocable.

A closely related subject is that of bond rights and warrants. Generally, when a shareholder receives rights to subscribe to bonds that are convertible into shares of stock, the rights will be nontaxable if a dividend paid on the stock into which the bonds are convertible would be a nontaxable stock dividend and the value of the rights is attributable to the conversion privilege. The basis is determined in the same manner as if it were new stock. Should the bonds be converted into stock, the basis of the new stock is the basis of the bonds plus any consideration paid at the time of the conversion. If the bonds are not convertible into stock, such rights are treated as property dividends. The basis of the shares remains unchanged, and the basis of the bonds is determined in the same manner as that of new stock.

As noted previously, a distribution is not an ordinary dividend if it is not paid out of the corporation's earnings and profits. In such cases it is treated as a return of the shareholder's investment. Such a return of capital is not taxed until the shareholder's basis in the stock has been fully recovered. To the extent that a return of capital exceeds one's basis in the stock, it is included in the tax return as a capital gain.

Stockholders receive a liquidating dividend when the corporation redeems their stock in a partial or complete liquidation. Such stock may be redeemed for cash or for the corporation's assets. For a partial liquidation of stock, the tax treatment depends on whether a redemption of stock held by a noncorporate stockholder is essentially equivalent to a dividend. If it is, the distribution is treated as a dividend taxable to the shareholder, but any gain on any appreciated property included in the distribution is taxed to the corporation. For a complete liquidation, the amount received is treated as the proceeds from the sale of the redeemed stock by the shareholder. In computing the amount received, any property received is taken into consideration based on its fair market value. The amount of gain or loss is the difference between the basis of the redeemed stock and the amount received in liquidation. Because the stock is a capital asset, the shareholder will have a capital gain or loss unless an exception applies (e.g., the collapsible corporation rules). Whether the gain or loss is short- or long-term will depend on when the stock was acquired and for how long a period it was held.

19

TAXATION OF THE ENTREPRENEUR

This Key will outline the tax treatment of the small business S corporation and the regular (C) corporation. The tax law allows S corporations to elect special tax treatment, so that tax at the corporate level is avoided. Instead, the income and expenses of the corporation are divided among the shareholders, who then report them on their own tax returns. Regular (C) corporations have their advantages too. For example, income splitting between the corporation and the individual can be accomplished through this form to shelter business income from the progressive rates applicable to individuals. Although the regular corporation still offers certain tax-free benefits (e.g., group life insurance) not available to other forms, the advantages to a small business of operating as a regular corporation may be more apparent than real, in view of changes in the Internal Revenue Code.

Federal law imposes a tax on the taxable income of every corporation without defining the term. The Internal Revenue Code's definitional section states that the term *corporation* includes associations, joint stock companies, and insurance companies. The fact that a corporation is treated as such under state law is not necessarily determinative, since the IRS classification is based on federal and not on state law. Under federal tax law, a corporation is an entity with associates, an objective of carrying on a business for profit and dividing the gains therefrom, continuity of life, centralized management, limited liability, and free transferability of interests. Sole proprietorships, business partnerships, and most trusts are not classified as corporations because they do not meet these criteria. (Note: The check-the-box system of entity classification has greatly simplified this process.)

The S corporation law enables the owners of closely held corporations to avoid the double taxation of business income—once at the corporate level and again at the shareholder level—without loss of the corporate advantage of limited liability. S corporations are like partnerships in that most of the tax attributes pass through to the individual shareholders and are reported by them on their respective tax returns. If the business should experience losses, S corporation status allows the shareholders to use them to offset or shelter their other income. At-risk rules limit the amount of losses deductible by shareholders to the shareholder's basis in the stock, including such items as loans that the shareholder makes to the corporation and the net fair market value of personal assets that secure nonrecourse borrowing. Thus, the at-risk rules effectively limit a taxpayer's deductible losses to the amount that is at risk and that could actually be lost from the activity involved. A taxpayer is deemed to be at risk to the extent of cash and the adjusted basis of property contributed to the business activity as well as to the extent of loans on which the taxpayer is personally liable or has supplied collateral. Although most regular (C) corporations are exempt from the at-risk limitations, personal service corporations and closely held corporations are subject to them. The at-risk rules were intended to prevent taxpayers from creating loss deductions. (Under prior law, a taxpayer could deduct losses created with nonrecourse financing, for which the taxpayer was not personally liable.) It should be noted that an exception to the at-risk rules applies for real estate secured by qualified financing. To qualify, however, the loan generally must be from a commercial lender and secured by realty used in the activity. Related-party losses may also qualify if the terms imposed are similar to those contained in other commercial loans.

The passive activity loss rules limiting the deductibility of business losses also apply to S corporation shareholders who do not materially participate in the corporation's trade or business, if no exceptions to the passive loss rules apply. Thus, such taxpayers can only offset losses of the business against other passive income (e.g., from the rental of property). Shareholders who materially participate in the S corporation's business can use their passive losses (and credits) to offset nonpassive income.

Note that if a closely held corporation—or personal service corporation—fails the material participation test, the company will be subject to the same passive loss restrictions as apply to individual taxpayers generally (i.e., passive losses are deductible only to the extent of passive income so that passive losses may not offset ordinary or portfolio income). Also, if a self-employed individual conducts an activity that qualifies as a trade or business carried on for profit, income and expenses from the proprietorship are reported on Schedule C of Form 1040. However, all losses incurred are fully deductible, albeit subject to the at-risk and passive activity loss limitations set forth above. An activity operating without a profit motive is subject to the hobby loss rules and is not reported on Schedule C of Form 1040. The expenses from the activity are deductible only to the extent of gross income—reduced by expenses incurred that are otherwise allowable without regard to profit motive, and then by expenses incurred that would be deductible if the activity was engaged in for profit, but that do not result in an adjustment to the basis of the property (e.g., advertising expense). In sum, the ability to deduct losses will be limited if the IRS considers the business to be a hobby, with such expenses being deductible only to the extent of the income from the hobby. Thus, hobby losses cannot be used to offset other kinds of income. Although the IRS is not limited in the kinds of businesses it can challenge as being hobbies, businesses that look like hobbies, such as auto racing and cattle breeding, are more likely to attract IRS scrutiny.

An S corporation must file a return on Form 1120S each year even though it may not be subject to tax. It reports gross income and allowable deductions, as well as information regarding the shareholders, their holdings, distributions, and pro rata shares of corporate items. The S corporation must furnish each shareholder with a copy of its return on or before the day the return is filed.

All S corporations generally must adopt the calendar year for federal tax purposes unless a bona fide business purpose for using a fiscal year can be shown to the satisfaction of the IRS. This ruling is intended to conform corporate tax years with those of the owners of the business. Thus, the use of a fiscal year by an S corporation is limited. Regarding partnerships, generally the tax year of a new or existing partnership must conform to that of the partners. If two or more partners have different tax years, the partnership adopts the tax year of those partners who have an aggregate interest in partnership capital and profits of more than 50 percent. If no partner or group of partners having more than a 50 percent interest in partnership capital and profits has the same tax year, the partnership adopts the tax year of all partners who have a 5 percent or more interest in partnership capital or profits. If neither of these rules apply, the partnership must adopt the tax year resulting in the least deferral of income to the partners. A regular (C) corporation meanwhile may select one of the following as its tax year: (1) calendar year, (2) 52–53 week year, or (3) fiscal year. A 52–53 week year is an annual period that varies from 52 to 53 weeks and always ends on the same day of the week, either: (1) on whatever date that day of the week last occurs in a calendar month, or (2) on whatever date that day of the week falls nearest to the last day of the calendar month (e.g., the third Monday in October). Note that the use of a 52–53 week year or a fiscal year offers the potential for tax deferral. Thus, if a corporation has a September 30 year end and its shareholders all have a December 31 year end, payments such as shareholder bonuses can be made late in the corporation's tax year but up to September 30. The corporation can deduct these payments on its September 30 tax return. However, the shareholders will not have to report the income until they file their own calendar year returns, creating a deferral of tax.

The Tax Reform Act of 1986 made three important changes in the taxation of regular corporations that affected the selection of corporate form. First, the law generally made the top corporate rates higher than the top rates facing individuals, so that a corporation expected to have taxable income of $75,000 or less might have been better off staying with the regular corporate tax form to keep those favorable rates. However, regular corporations, like individuals, became subject to a tough alternative minimum tax equal to the excess of the tentative minimum tax for the tax year over the regular tax. The tentative minimum tax for this purpose is 20 percent of the alternative minimum tax base reduced by the foreign tax credit on the alternative minimum tax and the regular tax liability.

In sum, a C corporation is subject to both the regular corporate income tax and the alternative minimum tax. A partnership or an S corporation is not subject to the alternative minimum tax, although the owners may be subject to it on their individual income tax returns. Each owner must perform the alternative minimum tax calculation to determine whether the tax applies. For tax years starting in 1998, small corporations are excluded from the alternative minimum tax. For this purpose, a small corporation is defined as one having three-year average annual gross receipts not exceeding $5 million for its first tax year beginning after 1996, and having three-year average annual gross receipts not exceeding $7.5 million for any later year. Again, this exemption does not apply to S corporations, which are not subject to the alternative tax. Thus, an S corporation passes through alternative minimum tax adjustment and preference items to the shareholders regardless of the S corporation's gross receipts. Note that a corporation that has been exempt from the alternative minimum tax as a small corporation and then becomes subject to the alternative minimum tax when it exceeds the gross receipts threshold will remain liable for the alternative minimum tax in all future years.

The reader might have been tempted to create as many corporations as possible, spreading out income in order to take advantage of the lower tax rates. However, a controlled group of corporations is allowed just one amount in each of the corporate tax brackets beneath the top bracket, which is divided equally among them or shared as they elect, along with a single maximum accumulated earnings tax credit. For this purpose, a controlled group is defined as either a parent-subsidiary group or a brother-sister group.

The second major change in corporate taxation brought about by the Tax Reform Act of 1986 provided for a corporate-level as well as an individual-level tax on the liquidation of a corporation. Subject to certain exceptions, the law provides that gain or loss will be recognized to a liquidating corporation on the distribution of property to its shareholders in complete liquidation as if the property were sold at its fair market value. Gain or loss will also have tax consequences for shareholders when they receive the liquidating distributions. The imposition of a tax on the liquidating corporation, along with the increase in the capital gains tax rates, more than doubled the maximum federal tax rate on corporate liquidations compared with that existing prior to the 1986 Act.

A third major tax change relates to net operating loss carryforwards. Before we examine this change, some background information is in order. First, every regular corporation must file an annual income tax return whether or not it has taxable income, and it must make estimated tax payments if its tax can reasonably be expected to be $40 or more. Corporations that receive articles of incorporation but never perfect their organization, transact business, or receive income may apply to the IRS to be relieved of such filing.

A corporation not in existence for an entire year is required to file a return for the part of the year it was in existence. This return must be filed on or before the fifteenth day of the third month following the close of the corporation's tax year. Corporations may receive an automatic extension of six months for filing the return if they file the prescribed form by the due date of the return. Corporations that are members of an affiliated group (those that are controlled through at least 80 percent ownership by the common parent and/or other members of the group, with the common parent directly controlling at least one subsidiary member) may elect to have their common parent file a single *consolidated return* for all of the members in lieu of separate tax returns by each. Note that every subsidiary must adopt the parent's accounting period the first year its income is included in the consolidated return. Generally, once a consolidated return is filed, the group must continue to file on a consolidated basis. A number of tax-saving benefits follow from filing a consolidated return. For instance, the operating losses of one group member may be offset against the operating profits of another. Intercompany profits and losses are not generally taken into income until ultimately realized in transactions with outsiders, and there is no tax on intercompany dividends. There are disadvantages to filing a consolidated return as well. For example, losses on intercompany transactions must be deferred, and consolidated income for tax purposes may differ from income for financial statement (book) purposes.

A new corporation can generally choose the fiscal

year that most benefits its shareholders. Assume that a corporation begins business on January 1 and elects a June 30 fiscal year. The resulting six-month deferral may reduce taxes significantly during the first year. However, personal service corporations are required to adopt a calendar year for tax purposes. (In such corporations the principal activity is the performance of personal services, substantially performed by owner-employees.) So, too, are S corporations, unless one of two mechanical tests is passed.

Gross income of a corporation, for federal tax purposes, consists not only of gross receipts from the sale of goods or services but also of interest, dividends, rents, royalties, and other "passive-type" income. Taxable income is gross income minus the deductions allowed corporations, so there is no "adjusted gross income" as is the case with individuals. As noted previously, a company's book income may differ from its taxable income. Some book expenses may not be deductible for tax purposes, and certain book income may be exempt from federal taxation. (The corporate tax return has schedules designed to reconcile book income and taxable income.)

There are significant differences in the tax treatment of capital losses between individuals and corporations. For one thing, corporations are not permitted to claim net capital losses as a deduction against ordinary income; such losses can be used only to offset capital gains and may be carried back three years and forward five years. On the other hand, corporate taxpayers generally have more recapture of depreciation than individuals, particularly when real estate is involved. In addition, corporations can deduct 80 percent (100 percent in the case of affiliated corporations) of dividends received from other domestic corporations. Although the deduction generally is limited to the lesser of 80 percent of the qualifying dividends or 80 percent of taxable income, an exception applies when the full deduction yields a net operating loss. The 80 percent dividends-received deduction for corporations is reduced to 70 percent if the recipient corporation owns less than 20 percent of the voting power and value of the payer's stock.

Note that dividend income is generally recognized and the allowance of the related dividends-received deduction made, as of the dividend's date of receipt, not the date of declaration. Further, when property other than cash is distributed, the amount of the dividend for purposes of the dividends-received deduction is the fair market value of such property on the date of distribution, reduced by any liabilities that are assumed by the recipient or to which the property is subject. Further, as is the case with cash, in order to be treated as a dividend, the distribution must be from current or accumulated earnings and profits. For example, a shareholder owns 200 shares of ABC Company, representing less than 20 percent of its outstanding stock. A property dividend is declared, with said property having a value of $5,000 and subject to a liability of $2,000. The fair market value of the property is determined as of the date of distribution even if the distribution is included in the shareholder's income on another date. The dividends-received deduction is 70 percent of the difference between the fair market value of the property ($5,000) and the liability ($2,000), or $2,100. Note that S corporations and partnerships are not eligible to claim a dividends-received deduction. Any dividend income that these businesses receive generally passes through to the owners without an entity-level tax.

Another deduction available to corporations is for expenditures required to organize the corporation. Under the law, a corporation may elect to amortize organizational expenditures over a period of 60 months or more, if the election is made in a statement attached to the corporate return for its first tax year. A standard election statement states that the taxpayer elects under Internal Revenue Code Section 248 to amortize over a period of 60 months all qualifying organizational expenses incurred commencing with the month in which the taxpayer began business. Organizational expenses include fees paid to the state of incorporation, accounting and legal services engaged to organize the corporation, and expenses incurred at organizational meetings. Nonqualifying expenses such as those associated with selling the stock are ordinarily added to the capital account of the corporation. Only expenses incurred in the first year are covered.

Corporations are permitted to deduct charitable contributions of not more than 10 percent of taxable income, computed without regard to the dividends-received deduction or any net operating loss or capital loss carryback. Any contribution in excess of the 10 percent limitation may be carried forward to the five succeeding tax years. A cash method corporation may deduct contributions only in the year made, whereas an accrual method corporation may elect to deduct contributions authorized by the board but not paid during the tax year if such contributions are made within 2½ months after the close of the tax year. A deduction will not be allowed if any of the net earnings of the organization that receives the contributions are used for the benefit of any private shareholder or individual.

The tax return must be accompanied by a statement that the resolution authorizing the contribution was adopted by the board during the tax year for which the return is filed. The statement must be signed by the president or other principal officer.

With the foregoing points in mind, we can now understand how corporate income is computed and how net operating losses can result. Generally, a net operating loss of a corporation may be carried back three years and forward five years to offset taxable income for those years. The corporation can elect to forgo the carryback and instead carry forward the loss. This rule is intended to allow companies to average income and losses over a period to reduce wide disparity in tax treatment from year to year. However, the 1986 Tax Act limits the amount of net operating losses that can be used when there is a change of ownership—resulting from purchases of stock, issuance of stock, redemption of stock, and so forth—of more than 50 percent of a company's value. The testing period for this purpose is ordinarily three years. In such cases, the net operating losses may not be applied against the taxable income exceeding the value of the company's equity multiplied by the long-term tax-exempt rate for the day of the change of ownership.

Regarding capital gains for individuals, the maximum rate on long-term capital gains is 20 percent, unless the taxpayer is in the 15 percent tax bracket, in which case the rate is 10 percent. However, beginning in 2001, long-term capital gains on property held more than five years will be taxed at a maximum rate of 18 percent (8 percent for taxpayers in the 15 percent bracket). This rate will apply only to property first put into service after 2000, except that for taxpayers in the 15 percent bracket, the special 8 percent rate applies to property first put into service after 1995. Note that if the result is a long-term or short-term loss, up to $3,000 will be deductible from ordinary net income ($1,500 for married persons filing separately). If the net loss exceeds this amount, it may be carried over. Partnerships and S corporations are not taxed on long-term and short-term capital gains and losses at the entity level. Rather, these gains and losses pass through separately on Schedule K-1 to the owners who report the same on their personal returns along with other capital gains and losses. A regular (C) corporation includes its net capital gain with its other income when it is taxed at the regular rates, although it may compute the tax on all other income at its regular rates and add to that figure an alternative tax of 35 percent of net capital gain. This is the alternative tax on capital gains and may be beneficial when the corporate tax rate actually exceeds 35 percent. Meanwhile, capital losses of a C corporation are allowed only to the extent of capital gains, with any net capital loss for the year treated as a short-term capital loss carryback to the three tax years preceding the year of loss. To the extent that it is not fully used in the carryback period, however, a capital loss is allowed as a short-term capital loss carryover to the five years following the year of the loss. Any part of the loss then remaining will expire unused.

Let's understand how this would affect the C versus S corporation decision. First, the rules relating to dividend income are unchanged, and since C corporations that own less than 20 percent of the paying company's stock can still deduct 70 percent of the dividends received, they have an incentive to remain C corporations. When it comes to the payment of dividends, however, the larger the dividend, the more likely that S corporation election will result in a lower tax liability. The reason is that dividends will be offset by lower C corporation rates only at the lower dividend levels. Second, as noted previously, many fringe benefits available to C corporations are not available to S corporations, and the rules respecting retirement plans favor to some extent the C corporation. The C corporation has more flexibility when it comes to election of a tax year, although, as discussed below, a C corporation may be subject to the accumulated earnings or personal holding company taxes. For state tax purposes, many states levy a tax on C corporations, but not on S corporations.

Next, because long-term capital gains generated by a C corporation are not accorded the special tax treatment afforded individuals, a corporation that expects to produce large amounts of such gains might do well to elect S corporation status. Thanks to the repeal of the *General Utilities* doctrine, S corporation status is generally preferable when it comes to the sale of corporate assets. The reason is that such status can reduce or eliminate the double tax on the sale of assets in a C corporation, although this benefit may be lost by imposition of the built-in gains tax. Simply put, the built-in gains tax is imposed on all C corporations electing S status. Although this tax obviously is not applicable to new S corporations, since they have derived no income from C corporation years, for an existing C corporation that elects S status, the tax is imposed on the net unrealized built-in gain on assets that the corporation owed on the date of election. An S corporation not subject to this tax might well wish to retain its S status, since any gain will be taxed only at the shareholder level and the shareholders will receive a step-up in basis, thereby reducing any gain on liquidation. Clearly an S corporation not expecting such a sale of assets might wish to revoke its S status.

For S corporations that are subject to the built-in gains tax and that expect to sell assets in the near term, the decision thus largely comes down to whether the regular corporate tax will be less than the built-in gains tax of the S corporation, since there is no current recognition at the shareholder level of C corporation gains. (Note: The C corporation can put off gain recognition at the shareholder level by not liquidating after the sale. Although this may subject the corporation to a personal holding company tax, in the case of a death of the holder of the shares, when the shares do pass to the estate and receive a step-up in basis, little of the gain would need to be recognized as the heirs liquidate the business). Of course, care should be exercised, since once the decision is made to revoke S status, it can be difficult to switch back. The law requires a company to wait five years before making a new S election, unless the waiting period is waived by the IRS. The tax regulations state that a change in stock ownership of more than 50 percent will induce the IRS to consent.

When it comes to existing C corporations, if the C corporation does not expect to sell its assets in the near term, S corporation status can substantially reduce any tax at the corporate level since there is no tax on the sale of assets by an S corporation once the 10-year recognition period for built-in gains has expired. (Note: The built-in gains tax applies to gains on the disposition of assets within 10 years of the S election.) If the corporation should sell its assets within the 10-year period, the built-in gains tax on the appreciation in assets will not apply because this affects only prior appreciation. The implication is that taxpayers should obtain an appraisal of the assets to be sold to limit the built-in gain that must be recognized on the sale of assets. This appraisal should include the value of all assets, including intangible assets, since otherwise it may be contended that the intangible assets (e.g., goodwill) existed when the S form was elected and the intangibles are themselves subject to the built-in gains tax.

This Key has thus far attempted to highlight some of the changes wrought by recent tax legislation as they affect the choice of entity decision. All in all, the net effect of such changes is still to encourage the use of pass-through entities such as S corporations. Whereas many factors affect the S versus C corporation decision, as noted, if the business expects to sell its assets in the near term, and if the company's tax basis in its assets is substantially less than their fair market value, an S election can help the business avoid the double taxation applicable to C corporations. S election may even be sought when the difference is not so great but there is a potential for future appreciation. Nevertheless, the built-in gains tax remains a trap for the former C corporation and should be carefully examined.

Two special problems will be addressed now, however, which are specific to C corporations.

A principal tax disadvantage of the regular corporate form is that the IRS may seek to disallow the compensation paid to shareholder-officers. Whereas the proprietor or partner may get used to drawing down whatever portion of the business earnings is desired, since he or she will pay individual income tax on the share of the business income whether or not it is distributed, and since the owner of an S corporation will be taxed on the share of the income whether it is taken as salary or as a dividend, it is only in the case of the regular (C) corporation that the temptation is present to inflate shareholder-employee earnings. Because the shareholder-employee is likely to push the edge of reasonableness, this activity will often prompt IRS scrutiny. This Key now considers two other dangers—the penalty tax on improper accumulations of earnings and the imposition of "personal holding company" status.

Accumulated Earnings Tax. The accumulated earnings tax basically provides that a corporation that shields its shareholders from tax liability by accumulating profits instead of distributing them may be subject to tax. The tax is imposed when there is an intent to avoid shareholder income and when the accumulations are beyond the reasonable needs of the business.

The tax is imposed on 39.6 percent of accumulated taxable income, which is taxable income after certain adjustments minus dividends and the accumulated earnings credit. (For this purpose, the accumulated earnings credit is the lesser of the reasonable needs of the business or $250,000 [$150,000 in the case of personal service corporations].) This tax is in addition to any other tax due.

A good faith belief in the need for the accumulation will generally prevent imposition of the tax. An important issue is whether the accumulation exceeds the reasonable needs of the business. Generally, the corporation must formulate plans that are specific, definite, and feasible rather than vague, uncertain, or postponed indefinitely. The plans should be recorded in minute books and reflected in appropriate correspondence. The regulations identify a number of needs that should meet this test, such as:

- Plans to acquire another business
- Bona fide expansion of the business
- Replacement of property and equipment
- Retirement of debt

- Bona fide business contingencies
- Redemption of stock
- Pending litigation
- Changing business conditions
- Working-capital needs

As regards this last item, the conventional formula for determining whether working-capital needs are reasonable is known as the *Bardahl* formula, which permits an accumulation equal to the costs of operating the business for a single operating cycle. (This cycle is often referred to as the amount of time necessary to convert cash into raw materials, raw materials into finished goods, finished goods into sales and receivables, and receivables back into cash.)

Certain corporate actions tend to indicate unreasonable accumulations of earnings. For example, the acquisition of assets unrelated to the corporation's business, the existence of large amounts of cash or other liquid assets, and the failure to pay dividends all favor imposition of the tax. Also suspect are loans to shareholders, relatives, friends, or others with no reasonable relation to the business, or to companies that are owned by stockholders of the corporation.

In light of the foregoing, what can a corporation do to avoid triggering this tax? Documentation is important. Thus, the corporation needs to identify the need for reserves for operating capital or for potential corporate liabilities and should justify in writing all decisions to retain earnings. The corporation should consider various means to keep its cash level lower, such as increasing inventories and not collecting cash from customers in advance. Further, whenever possible the corporation should employ outsiders to document the needs of the corporation to retain cash. For example, an expert might establish that, because of rising interest rates, the corporation needs to retain cash in order to reduce its debt.

Personal Holding Company Tax. A tax matter often confused with the accumulated earnings tax is the personal holding company tax, which was enacted to discourage incorporated "pocketbooks" from accumulating passive-type income. For example, a personal service corporation might be formed by a talented individual who would draw a modest salary. The corporation would contract out the talent's services at the going rate so that the difference between the amount received by the corporation and the salary paid could be accumulated in the corporate treasury against a time when earnings would diminish. The personal holding company tax was developed as a penalty tax to discourage such devices, and is currently levied at the rate of 39.6 percent of undistributed personal holding company income on top of the regular corporate tax.

For a company to be considered a personal holding company, it must meet two tests. First, more than 50 percent of the fair market value of the outstanding stock must be owed by five or fewer individuals at any time during the last half of the tax year. Thus, many closely held corporations will qualify, especially since very broad constructive ownership rules apply (e.g., stock owned by a corporation, partnership, estate, or trust is considered as owned proportionately by its shareholders, partners, or beneficiaries). Note that if 10 unrelated persons own equal shares of all of the outstanding stock, the ownership of at least six of the shareholders must be combined to constitute more than 50 percent or the stock ownership requirement will not be met. However, if the shares are not owned equally, then more than 10 individuals must be shareholders to avoid this requirement. Second, under the tainted-income test, 60 percent or more of the adjusted ordinary gross income (exclusive of capital gains) must be derived from personal holding company income. Personal holding company income is basically investment-type income such as rents, royalties, dividends, and annuities as well as income from certain personal service contracts.

If either of these two tests is failed, the personal holding company tax will not be imposed. One solution is to disperse stock ownership. Another is to reduce personal holding company income or to increase adjusted ordinary gross income so that the 60 percent threshold is not reached. Thus, the corporation might attempt to acquire assets that produce nonpersonal holding company income and accelerate the receipt of nonpersonal holding company income. For example, the corporation might discount its trade installment notes receivable. As a final solution, the corporation should consider an S election, since the income from S corporations flows through directly to the shareholders and there is no undistributed personal holding company income to worry about. For that matter, in an S corporation there is no accumulated earnings tax to deal with either, since all earnings are deemed to be distributed to the shareholders.

A further problem in this regard relates to corporations in the process of liquidation, at which time their operating income may be substantially reduced. By the time the corporation realizes that it has become what the IRS regards as a personal holding company, it may be impossible to issue a deficiency dividend, which is the basic remedy to avoid imposition of the tax. It should be noted, however, that a corporation may sell its assets and continue as a private investment company for the benefit of the shareholders. To avoid imposition of the tax, such a company would need to pay out its net earnings as a current dividend or, if it is intended that earnings be retained, to invest in tax-free bonds.

20

BUY-SELL
AGREEMENTS

In most publicly held corporations, the transfer of stock from owner to owner is a routine matter. But in closely held corporations there are generally some restrictions on stock transfers, in order to maintain the essential unity and integrity of the enterprise.

Shareholders in a closely held corporation may wish to restrict transfer (i.e., retain the power to choose future associates) for a host of reasons: preventing a competitor from buying shares, avoiding the loss of tax status, providing a market for the shares, or preventing one owner from purchasing a majority of the voting shares outstanding. Such restrictions on transfer make it possible to preserve the partnership-type status of a close corporation. Hence, the courts will usually enforce restraints that are not unreasonable and that serve a legitimate purpose.

Such restraints are valid and enforceable if the owner's consent to the restriction is found, expressly or impliedly, in the corporation's articles or bylaws, or in an agreement. Further, a transferee of a share of stock is bound by such restrictions if he or she takes the shares with notice of the restriction.

Under the RMBCA, the articles, the bylaws, or an agreement among shareholders or between the shareholders and the corporation may impose restrictions on the transferability of shares. The restriction will not affect shares issued before the restriction was adopted unless the holders are parties to the restrictive agreement or voted in its favor. Such a restriction is valid and enforceable against all holders if the restriction is noted conspicuously on the stock certificate or is contained in a separate information statement. The RMBCA provides that a restriction on transferability is authorized:

1. To maintain the corporation's status when it is dependent on the number or identity of its shareholders.
2. To preserve exemptions under federal or state securities laws.
3. For any other reasonable purpose.

When reviewing a share transfer restriction for reasonableness, the courts consider a variety of factors, including the size of the corporation, the degree of restraint, the duration of the restriction, the likelihood of harm to the corporation should the restriction not be upheld, and the efficacy of the restriction in relation to stated corporate purposes.

The RMBCA provides that such a restriction may:

1. Obligate the shareholder first to offer the corporation or other persons an opportunity to acquire the restricted shares.
2. Obligate the corporation or other persons to acquire the restricted shares.
3. Require the corporation, the holders of any class of its shares, or another person to approve the transfer of the restricted shares, if the requirement is not manifestly unreasonable.
4. Prohibit the transfer of the restricted shares to designated persons, or classes of persons, if the prohibition is not manifestly unreasonable. As is the case with preemptive rights, "shares" includes a security convertible into, or carrying a right to subscribe for, or acquire, common stock.

A buy-sell agreement restricts stockholders of a corporation or partners of a partnership from freely transferring their ownership interests. Such agreements provide that such an interest in the business will be sold—or offered for sale—at a particular price to the others and/or the entity itself upon the occurrence of a particular event, such as the death, disability, retirement, or withdrawal of the owner. Such agreements serve a host of purposes. For example, a buy-sell agreement may help fix the value for estate tax purposes. A buy-sell agreement is useful for maintaining ownership in a control group and excluding outsiders. A buy-sell agreement is important when a small company has no ready market for its shares, and will offer needed liquidity to the heirs of a disabled or deceased owner.

Various methods may be useful for valuing interests in closely held businesses. Since, in most agreements, it is only a partial ownership interest that is being valued, a business valuation consultant may be retained for this purpose. Under the *fixed-price method*, the owners determine the value of the business and assign a fixed price to the ownership interests. Generally, the owners periodically review this price. Although the method is simple, it may not realistically reflect the value of the business at the time of the triggering event (e.g., death of the owners). Under the *underlying assets method*, the owners look to the value of the assets of the business rather than projections of future earnings or cash flow. This method is frequently used when there is no earnings history, as is the case in a start-up company with little or no earnings to consider. There are three such bases—the book value approach, the net asset value approach, and the liquidation value approach. Unlike the other two approaches, book value can generally be determined from existing accounting records. The other systems require an appraisal to assign a fair market value or a liquidation value to each asset and liability. The book value approach is generally applied as of the end of the year before the triggering event occurs. The net asset value approach looks at the fair market value of each of the entity's assets and liabilities. The liquidation value approach looks to the expected net proceeds from a liquidation of the business after all liabilities have been met. To understand the foregoing approaches, some clarification of terms is in order. Book value is an accounting term that looks to the historical assets and liabilities. Liquidation value is based on the assumption that the company's operations will cease and individual assets will be sold. Fair market value is the price at which property would change hands between a willing seller and a willing buyer when the latter is under no compulsion to buy and the former is under no compulsion to sell, both parties having a reasonable knowledge of the relevant facts. The arrangement contemplates an arm's-length relationship between the parties. The third method used to value businesses, the *formula method*, is based on measures such as income, sales, and cash flow. An example is an industry formula based on a multiple of gross revenues or some other measure of earnings. Industry formulas are appropriate if the industry has a legitimate, recognized formula for determining value. Under the *appraisal method*, a formal appraisal of the business on a date specified in the agreement is used to establish the purchase price. The buy-sell agreement should establish how the appraiser will be selected and provide a means for selecting an appraiser if the parties cannot agree. Ordinarily, a professional appraiser is preferred—that is, one with formal education and training in valuation techniques.

There are basically two kinds of buy-sell agreements—stock redemption agreements and cross-purchase agreements.

Stock Redemption Agreements. Under a stock redemption agreement, any shareholders who desire to transfer their stock must first offer the shares to the corporation. On the death of a shareholder, however, the agreement obligates the corporation to buy, and the estate to sell, the stock. Statutory limitations may apply. First, a corporation's purchase of its own shares may be made only to the extent of unrestricted surplus funds.

Second, if the corporation is insolvent, or if the sale would render it insolvent, the corporation may not purchase the shares.

Cross-Purchase Agreements. In a cross-purchase plan, the corporation itself is not a party to the agreement. If the agreement covers sales within the lifetime of the shareholder, it typically provides that shareholders must first offer their shares to the other shareholders (generally in proportion to each stockholder's ownership). Upon the death of a shareholder, the agreement generally obligates the estate to sell, and the remaining shareholders to purchase, the stock of the deceased shareholder. Again, the arrangement would be in proportion to the owner's stockholdings.

Combined Agreements. In some cases, a combined agreement may be used. For example, the agreement could provide that a shareholder desiring to transfer shares must first offer the stock to the other shareholders. If they do not purchase the full amount, the shareholder must then offer the remainder to the corporation. The same kind of arrangement may take effect at the death of the shareholder. The agreement could provide that stock not purchased by the remaining shareholders would have to be purchased by the corporation.

Whether the agreement be stock redemption, cross-purchase, or combination, the agreement must have a bona fide business purpose, and careful consideration should be given to whether the corporation or the remaining shareholders are likely to have sufficient funds to exercise their rights or to perform their obligations. Although a number of options are possible (e.g., creation of a sinking fund), life insurance is often used for this purpose. This can prove to be very complex where numerous stockholders are involved, since a policy must be obtained on the life of every shareholder. For example, if there are 10 shareholders and they enter into a cross-purchase agreement, 90 separate policies would be needed. However, in a stock redemption agreement, the corporation takes out only one policy on the life of each shareholder.

Note: A corporation should never redeem any shares that the remaining shareholders are obligated to buy, because this may be considered a constructive dividend to such shareholders if the obligation is unconditional. Further, whenever an agreement calls for both a redemption and a purchase of stock by the remaining shareholders, the shareholders should be certain to purchase their shares first so that the redemption will qualify as a complete termination of interest.

Regardless of the form of the agreement, if properly drafted, the agreement can ensure the orderly transfer of that interest to whomever the owner desires, without an interruption. Again, the agreement creates a market for the shareholder's interest by protecting the corporation's existence as a going concern, and the remaining shareholders are also spared apprehension over the future. From a tax standpoint, it depends on whether the agreement is structured as a sale to the other shareholders or a redemption by the corporation. When stock is sold the transaction is treated as the sale of a capital asset—thus, the seller's basis in the stock reduces the gain on the sale and the capital gain is taxed at a maximum rate of 20 percent. If the transaction is treated as a redemption, and it qualifies as a sale or exchange, the gain will also be subject to a maximum rate of 20 percent. If the redemption does not qualify as a sale or exchange, however, dividend treatment results to the extent of earnings and profits at a maximum rate of 39.6 percent.

21

PREEMPTIVE RIGHTS

Preemptive rights protect shareholders from dilution of their interests when the board of directors votes to issue additional stock. These rights entitle all holders to acquire a proportionate share of additional shares of the corporation if such new shares would adversely affect their voting or dividend rights. Thus, if: (1) a corporation has 1,000 shares authorized, issued, and outstanding, of which 100 shares (or 10 percent) are owned by Jones; (2) the articles are amended to increase the authorized shares to 1,500; and (3) all 500 additional shares will be issued, then if Jones has a preemptive right, he will be eligible to buy 10 percent of the additional shares (here 50 shares). Of course, Jones must pay whatever price the board in the exercise of its business judgment has established for the shares.

Note that a preemptive right does not force a shareholder to purchase the shares. However, a failure to exercise that right within a reasonable amount of time following receipt of notice may constitute a waiver of the right, but only as to the offered shares. Once a shareholder waives a preemptive right, the corporation may generally sell the shares to anyone. Preemptive rights are especially important in closely held corporations, since the majority interest may attempt to "freeze out" the minority interest. In such a freeze-out, the minority shareholders' interests are reduced to relative unimportance against their wishes. Preemptive rights are far from a panacea, however. Thus, minority shareholders can be frozen out if they do not have the money actually to purchase the shares. Further, when a number of shareholders are involved, the effect of preemptive rights on future operations should be considered before any provision for them is included in the articles.

Preemptive rights vary according to state law. As these laws now stand, some states favor preemptive rights, whereas others allow them only if there is a specific provision for such rights in the articles of incorporation. The RMBCA provides that the shareholders do not have the right to acquire a corporation's unissued shares except as specified in the articles. The RMBCA makes it clear that a statement in the articles, "The corporation elects to have preemptive rights" (or words to that effect), means that the following principles shall apply, except to the extent that the articles provide otherwise:

1. The shareholders of the corporation have a preemptive right, granted on uniform terms and conditions prescribed by the board, to acquire proportional amounts of the corporation's unissued shares upon the decision of the board to issue them.

2. Shareholders may waive their preemptive rights, and a waiver evidenced by a written statement is irrevocable even if it is not supported by consideration.

3. There is no preemptive right with respect to shares issued as compensation, shares issued to satisfy conversion, option rights created to provide compensation, shares authorized in the articles that are issued within six months from the effective date of incorporation, or shares sold otherwise than for money.

4. Holders of shares of any class without general voting rights but with preferential rights to distributions or assets have no preemptive rights with respect to shares of any class.

5. Holders of shares of any class with general voting

rights but without preferential rights to distributions or assets have no preemptive rights with respect to shares of any class with preferential rights unless the shares with such rights are convertible into, or carry a right to subscribe for or acquire, shares without preferential rights.

6. Shares subject to preemptive rights that are not acquired by shareholders may be issued to any person for a period of a year after being offered to shareholders at a consideration set by the board that is not lower than the consideration set for the exercise of preemptive rights. An offer at a lower consideration or after the expiration of a year is subject to preemptive rights.

A safer approach is to ensure that all shareholders in the corporation have a veto power over any increases in stock.

A sometimes overlooked point in the area relates to previously authorized but unissued shares that are later offered for sale. Some jurisdictions have held that preemptive rights do not apply to such shares, even though selling such shares means that the minority shareholder's interest will be reduced. However, if the purpose of the sale is to freeze out the minority interest, a court may still declare it to be illegal.

22

REDEMPTION AND REPURCHASE OF SHARES

At some point in the life of a corporation it may be desirable for the directors to authorize redemption of some or all of the corporation's issued stock. Since the terminology of *redemption* and *repurchase* is often confused, it is worth clarification here.

Redemption. A corporation may acquire some portion of its outstanding shares by paying a redemption price to the shareholders, who in turn surrender their certificates. Note that redeemed shares can only involve certain classes of stock, generally with the idea of retiring shares with dividend preferences so as to benefit the common shares. If only a single class of shares is outstanding, it is generally not redeemable, since redemption would give the directors the ability to eliminate the shareholders to whom they are responsible.

When a corporation is permitted to redeem less than all of a class of shares outstanding, ordinarily this must be done either proportionately or by lot among all shares subject to redemption. That is, it cannot be done on a discriminatory basis. In any event, once the corporation does give notice that it is calling in a class of shares, the call is irrevocable. Thus, the holders of the called shares become creditors of the corporation, entitled to enforce their claims as creditors. A corporation ordinarily has the power to redeem its shares only when expressly provided in the articles.

The holder of redeemable shares is not a creditor but

a shareholder and cannot force the redemption (e.g., if the corporation lacks the necessary funds for the redemption). In any case, the redemption price (i.e., issued price plus a premium) may be fixed in the articles or by the board. Generally, this price must take account of dividends in arrears as well as accrued dividends. Thus, in a stock redemption, the remaining stockholders' percentage ownership of the corporation is increased, although no stock was conveyed to them. As an example, if Paul owns 900 out of 1,000 outstanding shares of a company and if Jan owns the other 100 shares but does not have sufficient resources to purchase stock from Paul (who wishes to retire), then the corporation's redemption of Paul's 900 shares will effectively transfer ownership control from Paul to Jan even though none of the stock was actually transferred to Jan. If the redemption reduced the number of shares outstanding from 1,000 to (say) 100, then after the redemption Jan would own all the outstanding stock.

Repurchase. It is not necessary that there be a provision in the articles giving the corporation the power to repurchase its own shares, since a corporation is generally empowered to acquire, hold and dispose of (but not to vote) its own shares. Although many jurisdictions have limitations that preclude the corporation from using such power unfairly, a corporation is free to repurchase its shares on a nondiscriminatory basis. Repurchased shares that do not have to be canceled (i.e., shares reacquired out of surplus) do remain issued as treasury stock until resold or canceled, with the right to vote, to receive dividends, and so forth, when subsequently sold. This is in contrast to redeemed stock, which is canceled and withdrawn. Note that treasury shares may themselves not be voted, counted for a quorum, or issued dividends. Once the corporation decides to purchase its own stock, it must provide notice to the shareholders, asking them to submit tender offers or fixing a price. The shareholders may also be invited to sell just a percentage of their shares.

Under the RMBCA, the concept of treasury stock per se has been eliminated. All shares reacquired by the corporation are treated as authorized but unissued shares. Of course, such shares are not entitled to vote or to receive dividends. If the articles should prohibit the reissuance of reacquired securities, the number of authorized shares is reduced by the number reacquired, effective upon the amendment of the articles. Articles of amendment may be adopted by the board without shareholder approval and are delivered to the secretary of state's office for filing, setting forth the name of the corporation, the reduction in the number of authorized shares, and the total number of authorized shares remaining after reduction of the shares.

As a related matter, a corporation may at any time integrate into a single instrument all of the provisions of its articles and any amendments to the articles that are then in effect. Subject to state law, such restated articles can be adopted by the board without a vote of the shareholders. The restated articles are to be executed, acknowledged, and filed in the same manner as are articles of amendment. After the restated articles are filed, the corporation's previous articles are superseded and the restated articles are the official articles from that point onward.

If the corporation redeems its stock under specified conditions, the redemption will be treated for tax purposes as a distribution in full or partial payment of a shareholder's stock. This kind of stock redemption is defined as an exchange between a corporation and a shareholder of the corporation's stock for property. The shareholder's tax liability on a redemption is the same as if the shares had been sold to a third party.

The primary tax advantage of such redemption treatment is that the shareholder can recover the amount invested in the stock without dividend consequences. Thus, whereas a dividend is taxable as ordinary income to the extent of earnings and profits, exchange treatment means that only the gain is taxed—as a long-term capital gain. As a result of a redemption, the earnings and profits account of the corporation is reduced by an amount not to exceed the taxable share of earnings and profits of the distributing corporation attributable to the stock redeemed. If the corporation distributes appreciated property to the shareholder in the redemption (or, for that matter, as a stock dividend), the corporation is taxed on the distribution. If the corporation realizes a loss by distributing property, this is generally treated as a capital transaction, not subject to loss recognition. Note further that expenses incurred in a redemption are nondeductible capital expenditures. Also nondeductible are such expenses as stock purchase premiums and legal, accounting, transfer, brokerage, and appraisal fees.

Under Section 302 of the tax law, there are four ways to avoid unfavorable dividend treatment for a redemption. First, a redemption will be deemed to be not essentially equivalent to a dividend if it results in a meaningful reduction of the shareholder's proportionate interest in the redeeming corporation. Thus, if all shareholders get essentially the same thing, the redemption will be treated as a dividend.

Second, a "substantially disproportionate distribution will not be treated as a dividend." In such cases, after the distribution, the shareholder must own less than 80 percent of his or her total proportionate interest in the business before the redemption. In addition, after the distribution the shareholder must own less than 50 percent of the total combined voting power of all stock. (Note that the effect of this cutback requirement cannot be frustrated by a planned series of redemptions.)

Third, if a stockholder terminates his or her entire interest—voting and nonvoting, preferred and common—through a redemption, the redemption will also qualify for exchange treatment. It is apparent that such a termination would satisfy the substantially disproportionate test mentioned above. In addition, the former shareholder must file an agreement to notify the IRS of any acquisition within a 10-year period and must retain all necessary records relating to the redemption during that period.

Fourth, a redemption in partial liquidation is not a dividend. To qualify, any distribution must be made within the taxable year in which the plan is adopted or within the succeeding year. The basic point of this exception is that shareholders receiving assets in a partial liquidation should receive the same exchange treatment as shareholders in a complete liquidation. If multiple businesses are each operated in distinct corporations, one of the businesses can be liquidated in a nondividend transaction.

Section 303 of the tax law provides that redemptions used to pay death taxes qualify for exchange treatment. Otherwise, such redemptions might qualify as dividends. This rule provides an executor a way to redeem the stock of a closely held business when the stock represents a substantial part of the gross estate of the shareholder-decedent. Thus, the estate can be provided with needed liquidity and be protected from losses in a forced liquidation of property in order to raise needed cash. After a redemption, corporate surplus can be used to pay personal estate costs. The redemption price is ordinarily the basis of the stock. There are several conditions that have to be met in order to withdraw corporate cash or property to redeem a deceased shareholder's stock in a Section 303 redemption. For this kind of sophisticated estate planning, it is best to consult a qualified adviser.

As noted, a penalty tax is imposed on improper accumulations of earnings. Such accumulations are legal if the purpose motivating them is a good one; if the purpose is a bad one, the corporation may be assessed a penalty beyond its regular corporate taxes for the current year. The law provides that if the corporation accumulates assets beyond the reasonable needs of the business, that fact will be dispositive of the existence of a bad purpose, unless the corporation proves to the contrary by the preponderance of the evidence. In the context of a stock redemption to occur in a future year, the issue is whether the present accumulation of assets in anticipation of that redemption is an accumulation of a reasonable business need. When none of the stock to be redeemed is held by a majority shareholder, and the current year's accumulation is reasonable in amount, the current accumulation is for a reasonable need. When the accumulation is for funds that must be available to redeem a majority shareholder's stock, however, IRS scrutiny is much more likely. The reason is the potential for abuse if earnings are accumulated to redeem a majority shareholder's stock because majority shareholders can use their position to cause dividends to be paid currently, thereby decreasing the future value of the stock and the amount of funds needed to realize the future redemption. By causing the corporation not to pay current dividends, the controlling shareholder is deferring the receipt of income, and if the stock is held until death, is enabling the estate to cause a redemption of the stock or a liquidation of the corporation without any second tax at all! If the stock is includable in the shareholder's taxable estate, it will acquire a new basis equal to its then fair market value. Clearly, this kind of tax motivation fits within the prohibition that underlies the accumulated earnings tax, and close consultation with a tax adviser is warranted.

23

SECTION 1244 STOCK

A related issue to S corporations is the Section 1244 option. As a general rule, any loss sustained on the sale, exchange, or worthlessness of stock is treated as a capital loss deductible only against capital gains and, at the most, against $3,000 of ordinary income per year. However, under Section 1244, a domestic small business corporation may issue stock that will qualify as Section 1244 stock so long as certain procedures are satisfied. Owners of such stock are entitled to take an ordinary-income deduction for any loss sustained on its sale, exchange, or worthlessness. The loss deduction limit is currently set at $50,000 in the case of a single taxpayer and $100,000 in the case of married taxpayers filing joint returns. Thus, a taxpayer who acquires Section 1244 stock at a cost of $80,000, then sells the shares later for $5,000, has an ordinary loss on a separate return of $50,000 and a capital loss of $25,000. (But note that on a joint return the entire $75,000 loss would be considered ordinary.)

When the taxpayer's loss on the sale or exchange of stock is computed, the adjusted basis of the stock is generally compared with the amount realized. Although the yearly limit for loss deduction is as stated above, more than this amount can qualify if the loss is taken over a period of more than a year by spreading out the sales of stock. Note that once the stock becomes worthless, the losses must be recognized in the year of worthlessness, however.

A Section 1244 loss will be considered a business loss for purposes of computing a net operating loss (NOL). For purposes of deducting an NOL carryback or carryover, the full amount of the NOL will be deductible even though a portion of it is attributable to the Section

147

1244 loss. For example, assume that an unmarried taxpayer had no taxable income for years 1, 2, and 3, sustained Section 1244 losses of $20,000 and $40,000 in years 4 and 5, and had taxable income of $150,000 in year 6. Also, assume that in both years 4 and 5, the taxpayer had other business losses of $30,000. The NOL for year 4 is thus $50,000 and the NOL for year 5 is $70,000 (i.e., the sum of the Section 1244 loss and the other business losses), resulting in an NOL carryover in year 6 of $120,000. Thus, in a carryover year with multiple net operating losses, the $50,000 and $100,000 Section 1244 thresholds set forth above will not limit the NOL deduction.

In order to qualify as a small business corporation, a company must have equity capital of not more than $1 million. (Fair market value of the corporation's stock is not considered.) The stock must be issued for money, for property other than stock, or for securities, and the corporation must be actively engaged in a trade or business. Although both Subchapter S and Section 1244 refer to small business corporations, it should be emphasized that the requirements of each are totally separate and additional to the requirements of the other.

The benefits of Section 1244 are available only to two types of taxpayers: an individual who received the stock in issuance from a small business corporation and is sustaining the loss, or an individual who is a partner in a partnership that received the stock in issuance from a small business corporation. Section 1244 is not available to a partner who in turn sells the stock. To claim a deduction under Section 1244, the individual or the partnership sustaining the loss must have held the stock continuously from the date of issuance. The benefit of Section 1244 is not available on stock issued to a corporation, trust, or estate.

Section 1244 loss treatment is not available if more than 50 percent of the corporation's gross receipts during the five tax years before the loss were derived from passive income, such as interest, dividends, rents, and annuities. This gross receipts requirement applies only if the corporation's receipts equal or exceed its deductions other than those for a net operating loss and for dividends received. Further, stock acquired through an investment banking firm or from another person participating in the sale of an issue may qualify for ordinary loss treatment only if the stock is not first issued to such firm or person. Thus, if the stock is transferred to another, it loses its Section 1244 character, and assuming that the holding period is met, is treated as a short-term capital loss.

Although there is no statutory requirement to this effect, it would appear advisable to have the shares qualifying under Section 1244 to be represented by different certificates from those that do not. Interestingly, stock issued on or before July 18, 1984, had to be common stock in order to qualify for Section 1244 treatment, whereas after that date either preferred or common stock can qualify.

Before the 1986 Tax Reform Act, combining Section 1244 with the S election could give a shareholder the best of both worlds. By taking advantage of the S election, shareholders could deduct operating losses currently and offset such losses against income derived from other sources. In addition, Section 1244 gave shareholders maximum tax benefits from losses resulting from the sale or worthlessness of their stock. For tax years beginning after 1986, however, the passive loss rules require that S corporation shareholders who do not materially participate in the operation of the business may not deduct losses until they dispose of their stock. Passive shareholders cannot use loss pass-throughs to shelter income from nonpassive sources (be it active income, like salaries, or portfolio income, like dividends). Generally, passive shareholders are able to offset their losses only against income from other passive investments.

Nevertheless, it may still be advisable to qualify stock

under Section 1244, so that any loss not recognized currently from corporate operations but recognized instead on a sale or exchange of stock will be allowed as an ordinary-income deduction. Further, Section 1244 qualification offers a backup position for taking an ordinary loss in the event that the S election is terminated or deemed ineffective for some reason. In this connection, it is worth emphasizing that nothing is lost by qualifying stock under Section 1244, since it exacts no cost for the benefit given and no penalty for failing to qualify. Gains are still capital gains, since Section 1244 applies only to losses. Further, a Section 1244 loss is regarded as a business loss and hence is deductible from ordinary income. In sum, Section 1244 allows the deduction of an ordinary loss by an individual or partnership of what would otherwise be deductible only as a capital loss. This section converts these otherwise capital losses into ordinary losses to the extent of $50,000 per individual ($100,000, if a joint return is involved). Section 1244 will be particularly helpful for S corporations whose operating losses are less than the total investment, since there will be basis available to use as a deduction when the shares are sold or become worthless. For example, if you invested $20,000 in a new corporation, elected S status, issued the stock pursuant to a Section 1244 plan, and sustained losses of $5,000 per year in each of the first two years of existence, you could deduct the $5,000 each year as an ordinary loss, thereby reducing your tax basis down to $10,000. Assume that in the third year, you decide to sell your stock for $5,000, sustaining a $5,000 loss. Since Section 1244 applies, this will be an ordinary loss, whereas, without this section, it would have been deductible only as a capital loss.

In sum, only the initial investment for a direct issuance of stock qualifies under Section 1244, although additional stock issued by the company for a subsequent contribution may qualify. The shareholder should file a Section 1244 statement with the tax return describing the address of the company, how the stock was acquired, the amount and type of consideration paid, and the market value and adjusted basis of the property transferred for the stock. In order to establish the Section 1244 deduction, the company should maintain stock records indicating who received the stock, when the shares were issued and for what amount, and the consideration received. The company should also maintain financial records to establish the source of gross receipts for the preceding five years.

24

BALANCING DEBT AND EQUITY

Investors in a new corporation can receive stock, securities, or other property. Subject to state law, corporate organizers have considerable freedom in determining the corporation's capital structure—be it stock alone or some combination of equity and debt. There are advantages and disadvantages to both forms of financing. With stock, any dividend payments are taxable to the individual but are not deductible by the corporation. With debt, the interest payments are taxable to the individual too, but are generally deductible by the corporation.

This tax preference in favor of thin capitalization—high levels of debt in relation to equity—is reinforced by the fact that it is permissible for a corporation to accumulate earnings to pay off long-term debt, thereby avoiding the accumulated earnings tax dilemma. From the standpoint of many investors debt is generally preferable to equity, since as creditors they will not be taxed on the withdrawal of their investment when the corporation repays the debt, to the extent that they have a basis in the investment. From a nontax standpoint, there are advantages too. For example, in any liquidation, the owner-creditor will be able to share in the corporate assets along with outside creditors. If the investment is in stock, however, the shareholder's interest will be subordinated to that of the creditors.

Among the disadvantages to the heavy use of debt financing is the fact that a corporation may not be able to meet its scheduled interest payments, and thus may be placed in default. Further, excessive debt may preclude the corporation from being able to establish lines of credit with other lenders, since lenders get nervous when the corporation's equity appears to be insufficient. Note that, from a tax standpoint, if the corporation should fail, losses attributable to the stock may qualify for ordinary loss treatment under Section 1244 (see Key 23). By contrast, losses on debt are treated as a nonbusiness bad debt. Such losses are subject to short-term capital loss treatment and thus may be offset against ordinary income only to a maximum of $3,000 per year. The distinction here is that a nonbusiness bad debt is one unrelated to the taxpayer's trade or business, either when it was created or at the time it became worthless, and thus is deductible as a short-term capital loss, whereas a business bad debt is fully deductible as an ordinary loss in the year incurred.

Another problem with thin capitalization is that the IRS may be successful in recharacterizing the so-called debt as equity. In litigation in this area, courts have tended to take an all-or-nothing approach, so gleaning the relevant factors is important. Five criteria are especially relevant in distinguishing debt from equity:

1. Whether there is a written, unconditional promise to pay either on demand or on a specified date, a specified sum of money in exchange for adequate consideration in money or money's worth, and to pay a fixed rate of interest.
2. Whether the debt is subordinated to or preferred over other corporate debt.
3. The ratio (or portion) of debt to equity.
4. Whether the debt is convertible into stock.
5. The relationship between the holdings of the stock and the holdings of the debt.

It is important to note that in order for inside debt to be valid, it must be treated as such. Thus, the instrument should bear interest and obligate the corporation to pay both interest and principal on specified dates. There should be a set maturity date, but if the maturity date is too far in the future, the debt may be treated like equity.

Payment should not be contingent on earnings. The debt should be properly recorded on the corporate books and reflected as a liability. If the shareholders' debts are subordinated to those of the general creditors, the instrument will look more like preferred stock and is likely to be treated as such. Moreover, if a shareholder has personally guaranteed a loan made by an outside creditor so that the lender is looking primarily to the shareholder for repayment, the debt may be reclassified as equity.

Note that for instruments issued after October 24, 1992, the character of an instrument as stock or debt will be binding on the issuer of the stock and the holders of that stock, but not on the IRS. An exception applies for a shareholder who treats the instrument inconsistently from the issuer, if the shareholder shows this inconsistency on his or her tax return. This rule was intended to prevent issuers and holders from claiming opposite positions. For example, an issuer might treat an instrument as debt to obtain an interest deduction, but the holder might treat the instrument as equity to realize a dividends-received deduction.

In sum, the issuance of debt enables the corporation to pay the shareholder deductible interest rather than nondeductible dividends and to postpone the likelihood of an improper accumulation of earnings, and hence the accumulated earnings tax. Moreover, generally, the issuance of debt enables the investor to withdraw cash out of the corporation at little or no tax cost while still allowing the shareholder-creditor to share with general creditors to the extent of his or her creditor position against the corporation if the corporation becomes insolvent. By contrast, when the shareholder's entire stake in the corporation is by way of stock, the shareholder may lose his or her entire investment if the corporation becomes insolvent. Note, however, that the IRS has issued a stern warning that it will carefully scrutinize the issuance of instruments that purport to be debt but that possess characteristics that make them really equity.

25

FREEZE-OUT

In the context of closely held corporations, a majority interest may wish to move from controlling shareholder to sole shareholder status and thus seek to freeze out a minority interest by a variety of actions.

In most jurisdictions, a specified percentage of shareholders can dissolve a corporation. Following the dissolution, the former majority interest could form a new corporation to carry on the business. The minority interest may be able to prevent such a dissolution if the majority's objective—ousting the minority—runs contrary to the best interests of the corporation generally. (A suit would be filed by the minority on behalf of the corporation, rather than on behalf of themselves. This is called a derivative suit and is distinct from a direct action to redress an injury to one's interest as a shareholder.)

Any attempt to freeze out a minority shareholder by amending the articles to take away the voting rights of minority interests can also be resisted, since a shareholder's right to vote is considered a right that cannot be changed without consent. (Note: Although some changes to the articles are mere formalities, others may substantially impair the rights of shareholders.)

The majority shareholders also cannot deprive those in the minority, without their consent, of contractual dividend rights. However, they may attempt to freeze out the minority simply by passing on the declaration of dividends. Generally, the declaration of a dividend is within the discretion of the board of directors pursuant to the business judgment rule. Withholding payment of dividends for a long period of time can thus be an effective freeze-out strategy, since the minority is denied income

155

and the value of the stock may become depressed. The technique is especially effective when the minority shareholder is in financial straits and is heavily dependent on the dividend income. If the minority shareholders can show that the dividends were withheld solely to freeze them out, a court may compel declaration of a dividend.

If the dividend oppression caused the minority shareholders to sell their interest in the corporation to the majority shareholder below its true value, however, a different remedy is needed; the court may allow the minority holder, like any other defrauded seller, to rescind the sale or to recover from the majority shareholder as damages the difference between the price received and the fair value of the stock.

Thus, there are limits to the board's ability to omit declaration of a dividend, and a court may grant relief if the minority can prove that the directors abused their discretion by acting arbitrarily, fraudulently, or in bad faith. As one court has put it, "[The] courts will not allow the directors to use their power oppressively by refusing to declare dividends where the net profits and the condition and character of the business clearly warrant it." To determine if the directors have acted properly, the courts examine such factors as the firm's current and future financial needs and whether there are any indications that the majority shareholders have used their influence to harm the minority, or have particular interests (not shared with the minority shareholders) in keeping dividends minimal. Minority shareholders can avoid this problem from the beginning by executing agreements requiring the declaration of dividends under specified circumstances.

26

DISSOLUTION

Dissolution involves gathering together the corporate assets, paying the corporate creditors, and then distributing the remaining corporate assets to the shareholders. Note that if any corporate assets remain when the winding-up phase is complete, such assets "escheat" to the state unless the applicable statutes provide otherwise.

There are two principal methods of dissolving a corporation: voluntary and involuntary. In the case of the voluntary dissolution, state statutes generally require a vote of the board of directors recommending a plan of dissolution to the shareholders. The plan must be approved by a majority or a prescribed percentage of the outstanding shares, and there must be a filing of a certificate of dissolution with the office of the secretary of state. Many states require notice to creditors either directly or by publication. Of course, the courts may enjoin a voluntary dissolution if it is found to be unfair or designed to eliminate minority interests.

Involuntary dissolution may be accomplished by action of the state, the directors, or the shareholders. The state may act where there has been an abuse of authority or where a particular requirement, such as the payment of taxes or the filing of an annual report, has not been met. The shareholders may bring an action only if a specified percentage of the shareholders concur and there are clearly articulated grounds for dissolution, such as abuse of power, abandonment of the business, or misapplication of corporate assets. Thus, a corporation may be involuntarily dissolved when the directors or those in control have acted oppressively, illegally, or fraudulently toward the complaining shareholders.

As another example, "deadlock" can occur when the board consists of an even number of directors who are equally divided and unable to agree on the management of the business. In the context of the closely held corporation, deadlock often arises when the corporate structure allows a faction of shareholders to hold up an action if they disagree with an aspect of corporate policy. The term *dissension* generally refers to disputes among the shareholders so acrimonious that they make corporate relationships difficult and ultimately interfere with the successful management of the business. Note that dissension may or may not lead to deadlock and, ultimately, dissolution.

Notwithstanding its name, the act of dissolution will not ordinarily terminate the corporation. The reason is that it takes time to wind up the affairs of the corporation, to pay the debts, and to distribute the remaining assets. Under the RMBCA, dissolution begins with the filing of a notice of intent to dissolve; the corporation is actually dissolved only after the liquidation process has been completed. During the winding-up phase, the corporation continues to exist and to have the powers and rights of a corporation reasonably incident to liquidation.

There are some alternatives to the dissolution remedy. Under Delaware law, for example, rather than ending the corporation's existence, a court is permitted to appoint a "provisional director" to serve on the board until the court finds that dissension of the board has ended or alternatively that the situation seems hopeless. Another option that is more widely used in the closely held context is to rely on arbitration to resolve disputes. Again, this does not always work, but it has saved many corporations from a premature demise.

State statutes generally provide the extent to which directors and/or shareholders will be liable to creditors upon dissolution of the corporation. Ordinarily, there is no liability if the procedures for dissolution were carried out in strict conformity with the law. Otherwise, directors may be liable to the corporation for distributions to shareholders without making adequate provision for payment to creditors; to the shareholders for any distribution not in accordance with the terms of their shares; or to creditors, who may be able to pursue assets in the possession of shareholders if the distribution prejudiced their rights. Further, there are occasions when payments made to creditors themselves may be reversed if deemed preferential. At the federal level, preferential payments occur when a corporation satisfies certain debts to the detriment of other creditors. At the state level, one needs to consult any applicable fraudulent conveyance statute. Moreover, under federal tax law, corporate officers, employees, and others responsible for the payment of certain taxes may be personally liable for unpaid taxes following the dissolution of the corporation. Such tax obligations are generally not discharged in bankruptcy.

As noted previously, nonliquidating payments to shareholders are generally treated as ordinary dividends to the extent that they are distributed from the company's earnings and profits. When the dividend payments exceed the company's earnings and profits, however, the distributions are first treated as a recovery of capital from the shareholders' stock basis, with any excess treated as a gain from the sale of stock. This constitutes the tax treatment to stockholders. From the corporation's standpoint, cash and stock dividends generally do not create a taxable event, although distributions of appreciated property are taxable as though the property were sold at its fair market value. Although distributions of stock and stock rights are not usually taxable to the shareholder, a disproportionate distribution is a taxable dividend to the extent of the company's earnings and profits.

The liquidation of the corporate shell is a central step in many sales of small businesses. The corporation may sell its assets and then liquidate, or it may liquidate first and then distribute its assets to the shareholders, who in turn dispose of them. A complete liquidation results when the corporation distributes all of the assets in exchange for all of the outstanding stock.

The tax results to the shareholders are these: A distribution made in complete liquidation is treated as a full payment for the shareholder's stock, with the shareholder reporting gain or loss measured by the difference between the value of the assets received in the liquidating distribution and the basis for the stock surrendered.

Prior to the passage of the Tax Reform Act of 1986, a corporation was generally not taxed when it made such a liquidating distribution, which meant that the corporation did not report income when it distributed any appreciated asset, nor would it recognize a loss when it distributed an asset that had gone down in value. This was known as the *General Utilities* rule, after a famous case by that name. The 1986 Act repealed this rule, however, and a corporation must now report gain or loss on the distribution of assets other than cash in complete liquidation; the corporation is treated as if it had sold the assets at their fair market value to the shareholders.

If an asset is subject to a liability, or if the shareholders assume the liability, and the liability exceeds the asset's fair market value, its value is deemed to be the amount of the liability and the corporation recognizes gain to the extent that the liability exceeds the asset's basis. In like manner, a sale of assets in the course of a complete liquidation is generally taxable; the corporate seller recognizes gain or loss when it sells the assets, and the shareholder pays a second tax on the net proceeds of a liquidating distribution.

There are two important issues here concerning valuation and installment reporting of gains. The burden of establishing the fair market value of an asset rests generally with the distributing corporation, which must file Form 1099-DIV with the IRS for each shareholder to whom a distribution is made. This form records the amount of money distributed, if any, listing separately each other class of property distributed in the liquidation, describes the property in each class, and states the fair market value at the time of the distribution. For this purpose, the value of realty is usually obtained through independent professional appraisers; best estimates may be used for many other assets. When property is sold to an unrelated party shortly after the liquidation, the selling price normally establishes the fair market value, based on the fundamental IRS principle that value refers to the "price at which the property would change hands between a willing buyer and willing seller, neither being under any compulsion to buy or sell and both having a reasonable knowledge of relevant facts."

If a corporation adopts a plan of complete liquidation and, on or after the date of the adoption of the plan, sells property in return for the buyer's notes and completely liquidates within 12 months after the date of the adoption of the plan, the shareholder may report the fair market value of the notes on the installment method. For example, assume that a corporation adopts a plan of liquidation and sells all its assets to the buyer for $100,000—$25,000 in cash and the balance of $75,000 in five annual promissory notes of $15,000 each. The selling corporation has no liabilities and distributes the cash and notes to its sole shareholder within 12 months after adoption of the plan of liquidation. The shareholder's tax basis in the stock is $20,000. How much gain must be reported if the installment method is used?

First, the shareholder has a capital gain (long term, if so qualified) of $20,000. This is computed by taking the $100,000 sale price of the stock ($25,000 + $75,000) and subtracting the shareholder's tax basis in the shares of $20,000, leaving a gross profit to the shareholder of $80,000. The gross profit percentage is therefore 80 percent. The capital gain is computed by multiplying the $25,000 cash received by the gross profit percentage of 80 percent, to obtain a gain of $20,000. Since the notes are collected in the succeeding years, the normal installment method rules apply.

161

Thus, the installment method allows a taxpayer to defer recognition of gain on seller-financed sales until income is actually realized.

A couple of examples may be helpful to illustrate the effects of a corporate liquidation in the context of a business transfer. Assume that the owner of a corporation has decided to liquidate a company whose assets currently have a fair market value of $200,000. The corporation's tax basis in the assets is $100,000, and the shareholder's tax basis in the shares is $100,000.

If the corporation is liquidated, it will pay a corporate-level tax of $100,000, since the liquidation is treated as if the corporation had sold all of the assets for their fair market value (here, $200,000 – $100,000). At a marginal tax rate of 34 percent, the tax due to the IRS will be $34,000, leaving the corporation $166,000 in assets for distribution to the shareholders.

For the shareholder, a distribution in complete liquidation is treated as a full payment for the stock. The shareholder recognizes gain equal to the difference between the fair market value of the assets received and the tax basis in the stock. Since the shareholder's basis in the stock is $100,000, the recognized gain must be $66,000 (i.e., the $166,000 of net proceeds distributed to the shareholder less the $100,000 basis). This results in a $13,200 second tax to the shareholder (i.e., 20 percent of the $66,000 gain), leaving the shareholder $152,800 in after-tax assets. The tax adds up to $47,200, consisting of $34,000 in tax at the corporate level and $13,200 at the shareholder level. Since the gain was $100,000, the effective tax rate on the liquidation is 47.2 percent.

Prior to the repeal of the *General Utilities* rule, the tax rate on a liquidation was generally 20 percent, since the corporation could have been liquidated tax-free and the shareholders would have been subject only to a 20 percent capital gains tax on the receipt of the assets in liquidation. Since the 1986 Tax Act, the rate has been raised to 47.2 percent, assuming that the shareholder is an individual; for corporate shareholders, the effective tax rate is now 45.44 percent.

Now, consider a different example. Assume that the shareholder of a corporation has been offered $25,000 for either the stock or the assets of a corporation. The corporation has a tax basis in the assets of $50,000, but the fair market value of the assets is $25,000. The shareholder has a tax basis in the shares of $20,000.

If the shareholder sells the stock, he or she will recognize a gain equal to the difference between the basis in the shares ($10,000) and the sales price ($25,000), or $15,000. The gain is taxed once at a 20 percent tax rate.

Now, assume a sale of assets by the corporation, rather than a sale of stock. The corporation's gain or loss is calculated by subtracting the basis in the assets ($50,000) from the sales price ($25,000), for a $25,000 loss. If the corporation is liquidated immediately, no tax is imposed, but the shareholder pays a tax on the $15,000 gain—the difference between the cash received ($25,000) and the basis in the shares ($10,000). Thus, the tax effect is the same. Note, however, that the $25,000 corporate loss on the sale has been entirely lost and will evaporate upon the liquidation of the corporation.

What should the shareholder do? The answer depends on whether the assets have a low basis or high basis and what the shareholder would like to do with the cash. A shareholder who does not intend to start another business should probably sell the stock. The buyer could then use the high basis in the corporate assets to reduce the gain if the assets appreciate in value or to take the loss when selling the assets. The tax effect is the same either way to the selling shareholder. However, a shareholder who wants to start another business should have the corporation sell the assets, since the corporate shell could then be used (i.e., the corporate shell remaining after liquidation for tax purposes need not to be dissolved under state law). The gain to the shareholder on the liquidation is deferred, and the selling shareholder may be able to use all or some of the loss on the asset sale to offset gain at a later time.

Note that distributions in complete liquidation of a corporation may be effected through a series of distributions pursuant to the plan of liquidation. All the distributions need not occur at once or during the same year. However, ordinarily, shareholders receiving a series of distributions are allowed to recover their entire basis in the stock before recognizing any gain in a complete liquidation. Suppose that Carter has a basis of $100,000 in the stock of a company that adopts a plan of liquidation. Carter makes a liquidating distribution (to himself) of $30,000 in the year 2000 and another distribution (to himself) of $90,000 in 2001. Here no gain is recognized until 2001, when Carter realizes a total gain of $20,000. Note that a shareholder may also claim a loss on a series of liquidating distributions but only in the year that the loss is definitely sustained. Ordinarily, the loss cannot be recognized until the tax year that the final distribution is received.

The foregoing provides some idea of the issues involved in liquidating a corporation; other factors can play a role as well. Be sure to work with your tax adviser in this area.

27

A LOOK AT SECTION 338

Most buyers of small businesses prefer to purchase assets over stock. Although the process of transferring title to the various assets can be time-consuming, at least the buyer is clear about what is being bought. From a tax standpoint, the buyer can, subject to the strictures of Section 1060, allocate the purchase price to the underlying assets of the target and then take a step-up in tax basis to the asset's fair market value.

The corporate seller, however, may resist a sale of assets because such a sale is considered to be a taxable event, with gain or loss recognized by comparing the tax basis of the various assets to the sales price. In addition, the shareholders who receive distributions of the cash proceeds are subject to a second tax, regardless of whether the distribution takes the form of a dividend or a liquidation.

The buyer wants the step-up in tax basis that is possible with an asset sale, but the seller does not like the double tax resulting from such a sale. What about a sale of stock? A sale of stock by the owners is a one-step transaction that results in only a single tax on the shareholder's gain.

Since the corporation is itself unchanged in a stock sale, such a transfer has no effect on the basis of the acquired corporation's assets. The goal thus becomes to find a way to structure a stock sale so the buyer can still take a step-up in the basis of the assets. Under Section 338, which is applicable only to corporate buyers, a corporation may elect to treat a stock purchase as an asset purchase. This is known as a "qualified purchase." Specifically, a corporation acquiring the stock of another corporation may elect to treat the purchase price of the stock as the purchase price of the assets of the corporation being acquired (i.e., the acquiring corporation obtains a basis in the target corporation's assets.)

To qualify for such special treatment, the acquiring corporation must have purchased, during a period of not more than 12 months, at least 80 percent of the voting stock and 80 percent of the total shares of all classes of stock other than nonvoting preferred.

In a Section 338 election, which must be made by the purchasing corporation within 75 days after it acquires the 80 percent control, the target corporation is treated as if it had undergone a complete liquidation, conveying all of its assets in one transaction at the close of the day on which the purchaser achieved the 80 percent control (the acquisition date). The target is treated as a new corporation that has bought all of the assets at the beginning of the day following the acquisition. This is known as a "deemed liquidation."

Prior to the enactment of the Tax Reform Act of 1986, a deemed liquidation could usually be structured so that neither gain nor loss would be recognized on the sale of the target's assets. That loophole has been closed, however, so that a Section 338 election results in a double tax. The basis of the assets deemed to have been purchased by the new target depends on the purchaser's basis for the target's stock on the acquisition date. Assuming that the purchaser buys all of the target's stock, the entire basis of the shares is allocated to the target's assets.

Further, the old target must recognize income to the extent that the "deemed sales price" exceeds its basis in the assets. The buyer must pay the tax, and the new target, as the purchaser, is regarded as a corporation with no tax attributes, such as earnings and profits. In fact, a prime disadvantage of Section 338 is that any tax attri-

166

butes of the old target not used in its final tax return are lost forever. Another disadvantage of Section 338 is that not only does the old target recognize income to the extent that the deemed sales price exceeds its adjusted basis in its assets, but the buyer cannot use its net operating losses to offset any gain which has to be recognized.

There is at least one case where a Section 338 election may be advisable: When the target's net operating loss approximately equals that of the gain anticipated by utilizing the election, thereby allowing a step-up in tax basis since the target is permitted to use its net operating losses to offset the gain from the Section 338 election. Note that any net operating losses that remain are lost.

Given the problems inherent in Section 338, however, buyers sometimes try to structure a stock deal as an asset deal allowing basis step-up for tax purposes. This may be possible under a Section 338(h)(10) election, in which a buyer and seller, under specified circumstances, jointly elect to treat a sale of stock as an asset sale taking place while the target is still a member of the seller's consolidated group. Following the sale, the target is treated as if it had been liquidated into the seller. In other words, the target is treated as if it had sold all of its assets to the buyer, although, in reality, the target's corporate parent has sold the target's stock to the buyer. The effect is that the seller is not taxed on the gain from the actual stock sale but from the deemed sale.

In sum, under Section 338(h)(10) the sale of the stock is treated as an asset sale to the buyer and the buyer receives a step-up in basis in the target's assets. The seller, meanwhile, is responsible for paying any tax due, recognizing gain not on the actual stock sale but on the deemed sale of assets, that is, the deemed sales price minus the tax basis in the assets. (In a Section 338 election, the buyer is responsible for any tax triggered on the deemed sale.) The target is permitted to use any net operating losses to offset any gain required to be recognized. Since the target is deemed liquidated into the seller, any unused tax attributes of the target pass to the seller. (In a Section 338 election, the tax attributes do not carry over but are wiped out.) Section 338(h)(10) is a complex provision; the decision on whether to use it depends on the availability of net operating losses, the presence of tax attributes, and similar factors. In the final analysis, the decision between Section 338 and Section 338(h)(10) depends on who is the one with the largest net operating loss and hence the one best able to minimize the overall tax liability from the transaction.

28

TAXABLE ASSET SALES

This Key considers the sale of an incorporated business—essentially, such a sale can be either nontaxable (e.g., via a reorganization) or taxable. Taxable transfers are of two types: a sale of shares of stock and a sale of business assets.

For the seller, a stock sale is a simple transaction to effect and results in a capital gain, whereas the proceeds of an asset sale are ordinary income. For the buyer, however, an asset purchase is preferable, since it avoids the unwitting assumption of hidden liabilities by the buyer and, if the assets being sold have a high tax basis, there may be no corporate-level gain from the sale. If the seller has unused net operating losses or capital loss carryforwards, they can offset any corporate-level gain on the sale of the assets. In any case, an asset purchase allows the buyer to allocate the sales price to the various assets and to take a "step-up" or increase in the tax basis of the assets purchased.

Simply put, a step-up means that the buyer increases the basis in the asset being acquired to its fair market value. For example, equipment with a fair market value and an original basis of $10,000 might have been depreciated by the seller down to $5,000. In the case of a purchase of stock, the buyer would take a carryover basis of $5,000. In the case of a purchase of assets, however, the buyer can begin with a basis of $10,000 (subject to the allocation rules as set forth elsewhere). The buyer thus "steps up" the basis to the purchase price.

Thus, in an asset purchase, the buyer receives an immediate step-up in tax basis in the asset to the purchase price of the business. In a stock purchase, however, the buyer receives a tax basis in the stock being acquired equal to the purchase price, helpful only when the stock is ultimately sold; unless a Section 338 election is made, the buyer receives only a carryover basis in the assets obtained. Even Section 338 is not an efficient way to overcome this inherent disadvantage of a stock sale, since all of the built-in gain in the selling company's assets will be taxable to the corporation, and the benefits of any upward adjustments in the bases of depreciable assets or inventory will be recognized only over time. Therefore, a Section 338 election is likely to be advantageous only when the seller has loss or credit carryovers that can be utilized. The general rule is that when the fair market value of the assets being sold exceeds their tax bases, an asset purchase is advisable; if the tax bases of the assets exceed their fair market value, a stock purchase is preferable.

From the standpoint of the corporate seller, the subsequent liquidation of the corporation following an asset sale results in the corporation paying tax on the excess of the fair market value of the various corporate assets over their respective tax bases, and in the corporate shareholders paying tax on the difference between the proceeds paid to them and their tax bases in the stock. Of course, if the corporation is not liquidated following the sale of the assets and the corporate "shell" is kept alive, this second tax will be avoided.

However, the personal holding company tax may apply to such inactive companies, so caution is warranted. Specifically, under Section 541, personal holding companies are subject to an additional tax of 39.6 percent on undistributed personal holding company income. This tax can be avoided if the corporation distributes as dividends all of its after-tax income or if the corporation invests substantially in real estate or in tax-free bonds or stock where the interest can accumulate without being subject to the tax; even so, the corporation may be subject to the accumulated earnings tax under Section 531.

Still, keeping the company alive is worth considering for those shareholders who have a low tax basis in their shares and wish to avoid the large tax that would occur if they immediately liquidated the company.

In any event, in the case of a sale of shares outright, the seller of those stocks, whether corporate or noncorporate, pays only a single tax on the difference between the proceeds received for the shares and the tax bases of the shares. Further, in general, the sale of stock results in a capital gain or loss to the seller, which is problematic in view of the limitations applicable to capital losses. Fortunately, under Section 1244, a loss on the sale of Section 1244 stock is treated as an ordinary, rather than as a capital, loss. For Section 1244 purposes, the initial capital invested in the company cannot exceed $1 million and the corporation must have derived more than 50 percent of its aggregate gross receipts for the past five years from sources other than investment activities. Although the tax attributes of the acquired corporation generally carry over in a stock purchase, Section 382 provides an exception to this rule. Under this section, if there has been an ownership change, the income that can be offset by net operating loss (NOL) carryovers is limited to the value of the loss corporation immediately before the change, multiplied by the long-term tax-exempt rate. The net operating loss is available only if the acquired corporation continues in the same business for at least two years; if it does not, the carryover is lost.

The procedures differ somewhat for a taxable acquisition of assets and of stock. In a taxable asset acquisition, the buyer needs to obtain appraisals of the seller's assets pursuant to Section 1060 in order to allocate the purchase price, and the asset sale must be reported to the IRS on Form 8594. The seller's board of directors holds a meeting to authorize the sale of the assets, and the buyer or the buyer's board meets to authorize the purchase. The agreement is then executed, subject to approval by the selling company's shareholders. Subject to state law, those who disagree with the proposed transaction may be given appraisal rights that require the valuation of their shares. (Under the RMBCA, a shareholder is entitled to dissent from, and obtain payment of, the fair value of his or her shares in the event of certain mergers, share exchanges, amendments to the corporate articles, or the sale or exchange of all, or substantially all, of the corporate property other than in the usual and regular course of business if the shareholder is entitled to vote on the sale or exchange.)

Assuming that the parties do agree to the terms of the asset transfer, a bill of sale will be executed at the closing in exchange for the purchase price. If the selling corporation is liquidated, it will distribute its assets to the shareholders in exchange for the shareholders' stock, which is then canceled. The corporation must then notify the IRS within 30 days after approval of the liquidation by filing Form 966, as well as satisfy any state law requirements respecting liquidation and provide tax information for its final corporate tax return in accordance with IRS regulations.

In the case of a taxable acquisition of stock, the buyer deals directly with the shareholders. After the buyer or the buyer's board has approved the purchase, a stock purchase agreement is executed. The actual endorsement of the shares and issuance of new shares is relatively simple; the tax problem with a stock sale is that the buyer retains a carryover basis in the assets acquired, which generally translates to a lower basis than would be the case with an asset purchase. To avoid this, a "deemed asset" sale under Section 338, which does allow a step-up in tax basis in the seller's assets, might be considered. Section 338, which applies only to corporate purchasers, provides that, if the stock of a corporation (target) is acquired by such a buyer in a qualified stock purchase, the purchasing corporation may elect to treat the seller as if it had sold, in a single transaction, all of its assets (as old target) and then purchased those assets (as new target). The new target is deemed to have purchased those assets at the beginning of the day following the acquisition date. Put somewhat differently, if an election under Section 338 is made, the purchased corporation is treated as if it had sold all its assets at their fair market value, so the purchaser may obtain the fair market basis in assets even if the transaction is a stock purchase.

If Section 338 is elected, it is necessary to obtain appraisals. As noted earlier, there are problems with Section 338, so the Section 338(h)(10) election should be considered, in which case the buyer will get a step-up in tax basis of the assets but face fewer tax problems. In any event, at the closing, the stock of the shareholders will be exchanged for cash or other property. If the purchasing corporation decides to liquidate the new subsidiary, the seller's board must approve this and obtain any necessary shareholder approvals. Again, Form 966 must be filed with the IRS, state law requirements must be satisfied, and the information on the final corporate tax return must be provided.

As noted, the sale of all the assets of a business for a lump sum is considered by the IRS to be a sale of each asset and not the sale of a single capital asset. The buyer must allocate the total sales price paid among the assets acquired to determine the basis of the asset acquired. The seller, in turn, must allocate the sales price to determine the amount realized on the sale of each asset.

Prior to the adoption of the Tax Reform Act of 1986, the seller and buyer had opposite interests regarding the allocation of the sales price to an asset sale. The seller wanted to allocate as much of the sales price as possible to nonamortizable assets like goodwill and going-concern value in order to benefit from the capital gains deduction and to use the installment method for reporting taxable gain. The seller wanted to avoid allocation of the sales price to the depreciable and amortizable assets, because such an allocation would trigger depreciation recapture and the gain would be treated as ordinary income. The buyer, meanwhile, wished to allocate as much of the sales price as possible to the depreciable and amortizable assets to maximize later deductions; since no tax deduction was permitted for that part of the sales price allocated to nondepreciable, nonamortizable assets like goodwill, the buyer would have to wait until the business was sold again to realize any tax benefit.

Given the conflicting interests between buyer and seller, the IRS tended to respect contractual allocations unless they were clearly unreasonable or there was in reality no adverse relationship. This all changed with the enactment of the Tax Reform Act of 1986, which repealed the capital gains deduction; consequently, no tax differential now exists between capital gains and ordinary income.

When the law changed so that capital gains were taxed on the same basis as ordinary income, for the most part, a seller was no longer concerned with sales price allocation, because there was no advantage for the seller in placing a higher value on goodwill unless perhaps the seller had large capital losses to utilize. Congress understandably became concerned that the tax interests of buyer and seller would no longer be adverse. Faced with the possibility that the seller might be able to extract a higher sales price from the buyer in exchange for agreeing to the buyer's allocation desires, it enacted Section 1060, which applies both to the buyer's tax basis in the assets and to the seller's gain or loss on the sale of those assets. Section 1060 applies to actual asset sales; Section 338 considers "deemed asset" sales.

Section 1060, which is still in effect even though the tax rates have undergone changes, provides that the "residual" method of allocation must be used to allocate the sales price in any applicable asset acquisition, defined as any transfer, direct or indirect, of assets that constitutes a trade or business in the hands of the transferee determined wholly by the amount of consideration paid for such assets. Thus, Section 1060 applies not just

174

to the sale of assets of corporations but to the sale of assets of unincorporated businesses, partnership interests, and so on. According to the IRS regulations implementing Section 1060, a group of assets constituting a trade or business in the hands of either the buyer or the seller constitutes a trade or business for this purpose. Both parties to an applicable asset acquisition must use the residual method. Under this method, the sales price for the assets being transferred is allocated sequentially according to the assets' respective fair market values, based on which of seven classes of assets they are in. The seven classes of assets are:

Class I   Cash and cash equivalents.
Class II   Actively traded personal property as described in IRC Section 1092(d), such as publicly traded stock, government securities, certificates of deposits, and foreign currency.
Class III   Accounts receivable, mortgages, and credit card receivables that arise in the ordinary course of business.
Class IV   Stock in trade of the taxpayer or other property of a kind that would properly be included in the inventory of the taxpayer if on hand at the close of the taxable year, or property held by the taxpayer primarily for sale to customers in the ordinary course of a trade or business.
Class V   All assets not in Class I, II, III, IV, VI, or VII.
Class VI   All Section 197 intangibles except goodwill or going-concern value.
Class VII   Goodwill and going-concern value.

As noted, goodwill and going-concern value are identified as Class VII assets. For this purpose, goodwill is the value inherent in the favorable patronage of a business by customers arising from the fact that it is an established and well-known enterprise; the IRS has ruled that the presence of goodwill is evidenced by the potential of a business to generate a return in excess of the industry average on tangible assets. Going-concern value on the other hand, is the enhanced asset value inherent in a business already in operation. Going-concern value includes the capacity of a business to generate a return without interruption despite a change in ownership. One way to look at going-concern value is to calculate what would have been a fair return on such an investment during the nonproductive start-up period, a phase that was avoided by the purchase of a going concern.

Since goodwill and going-concern value do not have a limited life that can be estimated with any degree of reasonable accuracy, these intangibles are not amortizable capital assets with a current tax benefit. Under the residual method imposed by Section 1060, assets not falling in Classes I to VI are automatically forced into this category. Although there is at present no distinction between goodwill and going-concern value, there is still a good reason for separating Class VII intangibles from Class VI intangibles such as covenants not to compete, which are amortizable. This is a difficult task that requires the taxpayer to demonstrate that the amortizable intangible has a limited life that can be estimated with reasonable accuracy and is susceptible to a separate valuation.

The actual asset allocation is reported to the IRS on Form 8594. Filing Form 8594 is an important step in the acquisition. The failure to file this form or to include correct information may result in penalties. Therefore, even if the taxpayer has some doubt as to its applicability, it is a good idea to file the form in any situation where Section 1060 could apply.

QUESTIONS AND ANSWERS

What are the major forms of business enterprise in the United States?

There are three major forms: the sole proprietorship, in which one person owns the business; the partnership, in which there is an association of two or more persons engaged in business as corporation-owners; and the corporation, in which the entity, an artificial "person," is treated as separate for legal and tax purposes from its owners. Corporations range in size from one-person concerns to vast publicly held enterprises.

What do the words *domestic* and *foreign* refer to in the corporate context?

Subject to certain exceptions, a corporation is formed pursuant to state law and is considered to be a domestic corporation in the state that granted its charter and a foreign corporation in any other states in which it does business. The corporation is considered to be a person for purposes of the due process and equal protection clauses of the Fourteenth Amendment of the U.S. Constitution but is not so considered for purposes of the privileges and immunities clause found in that same amendment.

What are the principal characteristics of the corporate form?

A corporation has an existence separate and distinct from those who own shares in the corporation (shareholders). The shareholders elect the board of directors, who oversee the management of the business and appoint officers responsible for its day-to-day operation. Some important features of the corporate form are limited liability, centralized management, perpetual existence, and free transferability of interests.

What does limited liability refer to?

In legal terms, the doctrine of limited liability generally shields the corporate shareholders from the debts and obligations of the corporation. Whereas the sole proprietors and partners in a partnership (excepting limited partners in a limited partnership) expose all their non-business and business assets to business debts and obligations, shareholders generally expose only their investment in the corporation to corporate creditors and others seeking recovery from the business. However, the courts may strip away this limited liability (pierce the corporate veil) if shareholders tend to use the corporation as their "alter ego" or if the corporation was undercapitalized at the time it incurred its debts.

How is a corporation organized?

Generally, a corporation is formed by the execution and filing with the state's secretary of state of the articles of incorporation, which are signed by one or more incorporators. After this filing is accepted or approved, the corporation's internal structure must be completed. This is accomplished at an organizational meeting of the incorporators or the initial board of directors named in the articles. At this meeting, among the business items transacted is the adoption of the corporate bylaws, which govern the internal operations of the corporation. Unlike the articles, the bylaws are not made a part of the public record.

What is a corporation by estoppel?

In a corporation by estoppel, certain persons may be

estopped (prevented) from challenging the status of the corporation even though it is neither *de jure* nor *de facto*. Thus, a third party who has dealt with a purported corporation may be estopped from denying the existence of the corporation, and those who hold themselves out as operating in the corporate form are estopped from denying the corporate status. Further, a third party will be held to any agreement with the corporation, whether or not it is later determined that the corporation was never properly formed.

What is a promoter?

A promoter is a person who, acting alone or in conjunction with one or more persons, directly or indirectly, takes the initiative in founding and organizing the business or enterprise. Generally, the promoter discovers a business or an idea needing to be developed, locates people willing to make the necessary investment, negotiates the contracts necessary for the operation of the enterprise, incorporates the business, and assists management in starting the operation of the business. Generally, a promoter owes a fiduciary obligation to the corporation. Therefore, a promoter who conveys property to the corporation must disclose the price at which he or she obtained the property, and the failure to so disclose may permit the corporation to seek rescission of the transaction or obtain damages.

What powers are possessed by a corporation?

A corporation has the express power to perform any act authorized by law or its articles of incorporation. Examples include the express powers to sue and be sued; to have a corporate seal; to have perpetual existence; to appoint officers; to acquire, hold, and dispose of real and personal property; and to conduct business within and without the state of incorporation. A corporation also has the implied power to perform all other acts reasonably necessary to accomplish its purposes and not otherwise prohibited by law.

What does *ultra vires* mean?

An *ultra vires* transaction is one beyond the express or implied powers of the corporation. A transaction within the purposes and powers of the corporation is said to be *intra vires*.

What is the difference between a debt security and an equity security?

Corporations are empowered to borrow the money necessary for their operations by issuing debt securities. Such securities create a debtor-creditor relationship between the corporation and the securityholder and include notes (which have the shortest term), debentures (which are long-term unsecured securities), and bonds (which are long-term secured securities). Equity securities are shares of a corporation's stock, of which there are two principal types—common shares and preferred shares.

What is a share?

A share represents a shareholder's proprietary or ownership interest in the corporation. Ownership of a share signifies the right to receive dividends as declared by the board, the right to receive a portion of the corporate assets on liquidation, and, if voting shares are involved, the right to vote. Ownership of a share does not entitle the holder to an interest in the corporation generally or to any specific asset of the corporation. Title to corporate assets is vested in the corporation and not in the shareholders individually.

What is common stock?

Common shareholders generally possess voting rights and are entitled to dividends as declared by the board of directors and to a proportionate share in the distribution of assets on the corporation's liquidation. Because of these ownership characteristics, common stock generally appreciates or depreciates in price according to how profitable a corporation is.

What is preferred stock?

Preferred stock is a class of stock with a preference over other forms of stock, normally as to dividends, but sometimes as to voting or liquidation rights.

What is a stock subscription?

A stock subscription is an agreement by subscribers to purchase stock to be issued by the corporation. Such agreements may be entered into before or after incorporation. If the subscription is accepted by the corporation, the subscriber becomes a shareholder of the corporation. Unless provided otherwise in the agreement, subscriptions are payable in full or in installments at times determined by the board.

What form must the consideration for the shares take?

Subject to state law, restrictions may be placed on the kinds of consideration for which shares may be issued (e.g., only for money paid, labor done, or property actually acquired). Shares issued in violation of such requirements are void.

What price applies to such consideration?

Share value depends on whether the stock is issued on a par or on a no-par basis. With par-value stock, a fixed or stated value is assigned to each share. Such shares must be sold by the corporation at least at par value; shares sold for less are not fully paid and are said to be watered. No-par stock, which has no fixed value, was developed to eliminate the problem of watered stock and may be sold at whatever price is found in good faith to be reasonable by the board of directors.

What are the rights of shareholders?

Although shareholders generally do not have the right to exercise direct control of the corporation, they may exercise control indirectly through their voting rights (e.g., electing directors, amending the articles and bylaws, and acting on extraordinary or fundamental corporate actions such as mergers and acquisitions). Shareholders also have more limited rights such as inspecting corporate books and records.

What is the difference between straight and cumulative voting?

Generally, in all issues other than the election of the directors, a shareholder is entitled to one vote per share held. Straight voting would thus allow the holders of a simple majority of the shares to elect all the directors. To protect the minority interest, the shareholders may be permitted to vote cumulatively for directors. Thus, each share is given one vote for each director to be elected, so that minority holders can vote all their shares for one candidate or one set of candidates. For example, if a stockholder owns 500 shares of XYZ Company and four directors are to be elected, the number of votes that shareholder may cast in the election is 2,000. Under cumulative voting, the shareholder may cast all 2,000 votes for just one director or may divide them among two or more directors as desired. Cumulative voting thus enables the shareholder to have a maximum impact on the election of the board of directors.

What does voting by proxy refer to?

A proxy is simply a power of attorney given by a shareholder that allows someone else to exercise that shareholder's voting rights. Generally, unless otherwise provided in the proxy statement, a proxy will not be valid after the expiration of 11 months, and will be revocable unless expressly made irrevocable or coupled with an interest. In such a case, the proxy giver can be enjoined from attempting to revoke the proxy.

What is the difference between a merger and a consolidation?

A merger is a combination of two or more corporations in which one of the constituent corporations remain in being (the surviving corporation) after absorbing the other constituent corporation. A consolidation is a combination of two or more corporations in which the separate existence of the consolidating corporations is absorbed into a new corporation.

What is the difference between a *de facto* merger and a short-form merger?

A *de facto* merger contemplates a transaction that is structured other than as a merger but has the same effect as a merger. Such a transaction will be treated as a merger for purposes of affording shareholders a right to an appraisal (i.e., the right to require the corporation to purchase their shares at an objectively determined value). A short-form merger entails a merger of a 90 percent-owned or 95 percent-owned subsidiary into its parent. Generally, such a merger does not require a shareholder vote. Typically, the short-form merger provides that the minority shareholders of the subsidiary will receive cash only in an amount equal to the fair market value of their holdings in the subsidiary and that only the subsidiary's shareholders will have an appraisal remedy. All of this should be contrasted with mergers generally, which require board approval, shareholder approval, and filing with the secretary of state's office.

How are corporations terminated?

First, the corporation must be dissolved. It may be dissolved voluntarily before or after it commences business or involuntarily by action of a court or administrative action of the secretary of state's office (e.g., for not filing the required annual report or not paying the appropriate tax). Dissolution does not itself terminate the corporation but merely requires the corporation to cease its business, to wind up its affairs, and to liquidate its assets. Termination results when the corporation's assets have been liquidated and the proceeds distributed.

What is the basic tax difference between operating as a proprietorship, a partnership, or a regular (C) corporation?

A proprietorship is not taxable as a separate entity; thus, all of the tax effects are borne by the proprietor and reported on Schedule C, attached to Form 1040. A partnership is not treated as a taxpayer but as a tax-reporting entity via Form 1065, with items of income, loss, deduction, and credit passed through to the partners. As an example, consider tax-exempt income, which, if distributed to the partners, retains its tax-exempt status in the hands of the partners. In a regular (C) corporation, such income will retain its tax-exempt status only at the corporate level. A C corporation is treated as a separate taxpayer and not just as a conduit, resulting in double taxation. First, there is a tax at the corporate level on the corporation's earnings; second, there is a tax at the shareholder level on any portion of the corporation's after-tax income that is distributed to the shareholders as dividends.

Generally, what taxes are imposed on regular (C) corporations?

A corporate income tax is imposed on C corporations. The rates are as follows: for taxable income up to $50,000, 15 percent; $50,000–$75,000, 25 percent; $75,000–$100,000, 34 percent; $100,000–$335,000, 39 percent; $335,000–$10,000,000, 34 percent; $10,000,000–$15,000,000, 35 percent; $15,000,000–$18,333,333, 38 percent; more than $18,333,333, 35 percent. Note that only small corporations benefit from the lower rates. A 5 percent surtax is imposed on taxable income in excess of $100,000, up to a maximum surtax of $11,750—this is the tax savings associated with having the first $75,000 of taxable income taxed at rates lower than the 34 percent rate. Corporations with taxable income exceeding $15 million are subject to a flat 35 percent rate on all taxable income, as are personal service corporations. Members of a controlled group (i.e., parent-subsidiary group or brother-sister group) are treated as one corporation for purposes of the graduated tax rates. In addition to the regular corporate income tax, a C corporation may be subject to the alternative tax on capital gains, an alternative minimum tax, and two penalty taxes on undistributed corporate income. The latter penalty taxes—the accumulated earnings tax and personal holding company tax—may be assessed if a company retains earnings at the corporate level to defer the shareholder-level tax that arises if earnings are paid out to shareholders as compensation, benefits, or dividends.

What is the accumulated earnings tax?

The accumulated earnings tax penalizes the unreasonable accumulation of income within a corporation. A subjective test is used to ascertain whether there was an intent to avoid tax at the shareholder level. The tax is imposed at the rate of 39.6 percent and is in addition to the regular corporate income tax. The tax is assessed by the IRS and can be imposed on any corporation except an S corporation, personal holding company, tax-exempt organization, or passive foreign investment company. Unlike the personal holding company tax, this tax can be imposed regardless of the number of shareholders. Since there must be an intent to avoid income tax at the shareholder level by accumulating earnings in the corporation, tax avoidance must be one reason for the actions of the company, but it does not have to be the sole or primary reason. A tax avoidance motive is automatically present when the corporation is a mere holding or investment company or when the corporation has accumulated earnings for the year in excess of the reasonable needs of the business, unless the company by a preponderance of the evidence can prove to the contrary. Thus, a company needs to document the reasonable needs of the business when it has accumulated earnings. The following items are considered evidence of an intent to avoid tax: (1) a weak dividend history; (2) loans to shareholders (evidencing an ability to pay dividends or what may be characterized as pseudo-dividends); (3) investment in assets having no reasonable relationship to the corporation's business (evidencing an ability but not a willingness to pay dividends); (4) working-capital levels that appear high in relationship to need; (5) loans to other businesses controlled by the corporation's shareholders; and (6) illiquid investments unrelated to the company's business. A corporation is allowed a lifetime credit of $250,000 against the tax ($150,000 in the case of a personal service corporation) and is also given a credit for the reasonable needs of the business. To avoid imposition of this tax, the corporation should eliminate loans and other suspect transactions between the company and its shareholders, establish a regular dividend payment history, monitor the $250,000 lifetime accumulated earnings credit to determine if the threshold has been reached, and consider electing S corporation status, since the tax does not apply to S corporations.

How are reasonable business needs determined for purposes of the accumulated earnings tax?

Reasonable business needs that justify the accumulation of earnings include the following: (1) to provide for bona fide expansion of the business or replacement of plant; (2) to acquire a business enterprise through the purchase of stock or assets; (3) to provide for the retirement of company debt created in connection with a trade or business; (4) to provide necessary working capital for the business; (5) to provide for investments or loans to suppliers or customers if necessary to maintain the business of the corporation; (6)

to provide for the payment of reasonably anticipated product liability losses, actual or potential lawsuits, loss of a major customer, or self-insurance; and (7) to provide for a business contingency if the contingency is likely to occur. The corporation should have specific, clear plans to accumulate earnings, not vague, uncertain plans that are postponed indefinitely. An objective test called the *Bardahl* formula can be used to determine necessary working capital (the fourth reason above). Note that working capital required for a business is a function of various factors—inventory turnover, credit policy, accounts receivables, collection rates, and so on. The *Bardahl* formula relies on the operating cycle test. An operating cycle is the time needed to manufacture finished goods, convert inventory into sales and accounts receivable, and collect receivables. The *Bardahl* formula thus represents the cash needed for a single operating cycle. To illustrate, assume that a company has an inventory turnover of 75 days and an accounts receivable turnover of 25 days—for a total of 100 days. Subtract from this total the accounts payable turnover (here, 64 days)—for a net of 36 days, or about 10 percent of a full year. Multiply that 10 percent by the cost of sales and operating expenses (excluding depreciation) to obtain the working capital for a single cycle.

What is the personal holding company tax?

The personal holding company tax was passed as a penalty on undistributed corporate earnings and is aimed at incorporated pocketbooks. A personal holding company is subject to tax at the rate of 39.6 percent on undistributed personal holding company income. This tax is in addition to other corporate income taxes. A corporation is a personal holding company if it meets two objective tests. The first test is the stock ownership test. Under this test, more than 50 percent of the value of the corporation's outstanding stock must be owned directly or indirectly by five or fewer persons on any day during the last half of the corporation's tax year. Stock owned by related individuals, partners, and others is deemed to be owned by a shareholder. The second test is the income test. Under this test, at least 60 percent of the corporation's adjusted ordinary gross income must be personal holding company income. Personal holding company income includes the following: (1) dividends, interest, royalties, and annuities; (2) rents; (3) mineral, oil, and gas royalties; (4) copyright royalties; (5) produced film rents; (6) rents for use of corporate property by a shareholder; (7) income from personal service contracts; and (8) income from an estate or trust, if the corporation is a beneficiary. Since many companies will meet the ownership test, the income test becomes critical. A personal holding company may minimize or eliminate this tax by making actual or consent dividends. Consent dividends are hypothetical dividends agreed to by the stockholders and the corporation. In addition to the foregoing penalty taxes, collapsible corporations may prove troublesome for the closely held corporation and will be considered next.

What is a collapsible corporation?

Before the passage of rules on collapsible corporations, taxpayers often used the closely held corporation to reduce income tax for residential construction. The company constructed homes and distributed them to shareholders before the houses could be sold. The company was not taxed on gains on liquidating distributions unless the liabilities exceeded the basis of the property distributed. Current rules collapse the corporation as though it did not exist by converting capital gains into ordinary income at the shareholder level. These rules apply only to gain transactions, not to losses. Thus, a collapsible corporation cannot be used to convert a capital loss into an ordinary loss. The annual $3,000 capital loss limit cannot be circumvented by using a collapsible corporation. A collapsible corporation is one used primarily to produce property, and the rules apply only when the taxpayer intends to sell, liquidate, or distribute the property before two thirds of the income is recognized by the corporation. Companies with appreciated inventory are particular targets for collapsible treatment, as are companies with unrealized receivables.

If the corporation distributes $100,000 to the shareholder-employee as salary, how much will the owner pay in taxes?

Assuming that the salary is a reasonable one, there is no corporate-level tax (i.e., corporate taxable income has been reduced to zero). The shareholder pays tax on the full $100,000 of salary.

Since the tax law allows the employer a deduction for reasonable compensation, how do you determine what is reasonable?

In the normal case, you negotiate your compensation with your employer, so the compensation level is likely to be respected. However, in the case of small, closely held corporations, the IRS is more likely to challenge a salary as excessive and try to recharacterize deductible salary as a nondeductible dividend. To determine what is reasonable compensation, you consider not only the regular salary but all overtime, bonuses, commissions, and fringe benefits received. A number of factors are considered to determine if a particular shareholder-employee's salary is excessive, such as the time devoted to the business, job qualifications, comparable salaries in the industry, and past services rendered.

What penalties does the IRS impose for unreasonable compensation?

Beyond challenging the reasonableness of compensation, negligence penalties might be assessed. Since the excess compensation will be disallowed for tax purposes, it might be a good idea to consider a payback agreement. Such an agreement requires the employee to repay to the corporation any portion of compensation that the IRS disallows. To be legally binding, payback agreements must be properly executed before the compensation covered is actually paid to the employee. Such provisions should be documented in an employment contract and, when possible, in the corporate bylaws. Unfortunately, the IRS may take the position that the very existence of the payback agreement indicates that the corporation knew its compensation payments were not reasonable.

In a regular (C) corporation, when shareholder-employees are paid significant amounts, the IRS may attempt to disallow part of the deduction as unreasonable and excessive. Does this principle also apply to S corporations, partnerships, limited liability companies, and proprietorships?

No. S corporations, partnerships, and limited liability companies are all treated as partnerships for federal tax purposes, so the subject of excessive compensation does not arise because all distributed and undistributed taxable income is taxed at the owner-employee level. The same result applies to proprietorships. However, how compensation is structured in an S corporation can affect payroll taxes. The reason is that payroll taxes are due on employee wages, including salaries of shareholder-employees. By contrast, cash distributions from S corporations to shareholder-employees are not subject to payroll taxes or self-employment tax so long as the distributions are not really disguised wages. Since pass-through income increases the tax basis of the shareholder-employee's stock, the cash distributions are generally received tax-free by the shareholder-employee. The IRS thus may contend that the S corporation paid unreasonably low compensation in order to avoid payroll taxes, asserting that the so-called dividends are really another form of compensation. To see the dramatic tax impact of this issue, consider the following example. A shareholder-employee of an S corporation draws $100,000 as compensation from the corporation. The combined employer and employee payroll taxes amount to $11,009.60 (based on a rate of 15.3 percent on the first

$65,400 with 2.9 percent levied on the excess). If that same $100,000 salary is cut to $50,000, with the other $50,000 paid as a dividend instead, there is a reduction of $3,359.60 in payroll taxes.

What is a constructive dividend?

A constructive dividend is one recharacterized (generally in the course of an audit) by the IRS because a corporate shareholder was construed as having received some personal benefit from the corporation. Thus, amounts paid to a shareholder as compensation in excess of what is considered reasonable (as discussed above) may result in a constructive dividend. What is unreasonable will depend on both taxable salaries and nontaxable fringe benefits. Other examples apply when the company makes a payment for the personal benefit of the shareholder rather than for the ordinary and necessary needs of the business (e.g., payment of the shareholder's mortgage). A loan to a shareholder at a below-market rate may be a constructive dividend, as may be an advance to a shareholder that is not a bona fide loan. The shareholder's use of corporate vehicles or other property for personal benefit without paying adequate fees or having the company report compensation income to the shareholder for the fair market value of the personal use component may constitute a constructive dividend. Note that a constructive dividend is unlike an ordinary dividend in that no formal declaration as a dividend is involved, nor need it be considered a formal dividend under state law.

Assuming that the corporation distributes all its after-tax income to the shareholder-employee as a loan, what will the tax effect be?

Assuming a 34 percent rate, the corporation will pay $22,250 of tax on the $100,000, leaving $77,750 to be loaned to the shareholder-employee at a reasonable rate of interest. The taxpayer will not pay tax on the loan, meaning that the entire $77,750 is available after taxes. Years ago, shareholder-employees tried to borrow funds from the corporation on a zero-interest or low-interest basis. Owing to a change in the tax law, however, such arrangements now lead to the imputation of income; further, the IRS may try to recharacterize the loan itself as a constructive dividend. It turns out that in the case of a regular (C) corporation, it is better to borrow from a qualified plan. For such a loan to be approved however, it must be made available to all participants and beneficiaries on a reasonably equivalent basis; must not be available disproportionately to highly paid employees, officers, or shareholders; must be made pursuant to specific provisions regarding such loans as stated in the plan; must bear a reasonable rate of interest; and must be adequately secured. For this purpose, the vested portion in the plan participant's account can be used as security for the loan.

What is an S corporation?

A corporation automatically becomes a regular (C) corporation when it is formed; no special action need be taken. However, if the corporation, with the consent of the shareholders, makes an election to operate as an S corporation, the corporation will itself generally pay no taxes. Rather, the corporation's income, deductions, losses, and credits will flow through to the shareholders, who report such items on their individual tax returns. This means that income is taxed only at the shareholder level. Generally, an individual owner's share of an item is calculated by taking the annual amount of the item and multiplying it by the owner's percentage interest in the stock of the corporation. This means that if a taxpayer owns 95 percent of an S corporation that has a $100,000 profit for the tax year, the taxpayer's share of the income is $95,000. Note, however, that the income is taxed to the shareholder at his or her highest marginal rate. For example, if $10,000 of income were reported, the shareholder would be taxed on $9,500 of income, not at the corporation's tax rate of 15 percent but at his or her highest individual tax bracket. The S election must be filed on or before the fifteenth day of the third month of the corporation's taxable year. For a corporation to qualify for S corporation status, a number of criteria must be met: the corporation must be a U.S. corporation; none of the shareholders may be nonresident aliens; there may be only one class of stock, although differences in voting rights are permitted; all shareholders must be individuals, estates, or certain trusts; and there must be no more than 75 shareholders.

What conditions must be met to satisfy the "one class of stock" requirement for S corporations?

All outstanding shares must confer identical rights to proceeds from liquidations and distributions and the corporation must not issue any instrument or obligation or enter into any arrangement that is considered a second class of stock. Normally, all outstanding shares of stock in a corporation are considered in determining whether there is more than one class of stock. (Stock that is issued for the performance of services and that is also substantially non-vested will not generally be considered outstanding stock.) Whether all outstanding shares of stock confer the same rights falls within the corporation's charter. Note that debt obligations may constitute a second class of stock, but the law considers debt to be equity only when the arrangement constitutes equity or causes the holder of debt to be treated as an owner of stock. Further, if the principal purpose of an agreement is to circumvent the rights to distribution or liquidation proceeds conferred by the outstanding stock, such an agreement may be treated as a second class of stock. Note that short-term advances from a corporation do not constitute a second class of stock, even if the advances are treated as equity for tax purposes, so long as the advances do not exceed $10,000 at any time. The advances must be treated as debt by both parties and the debt must be expected to be repaid in a reasonable amount of time. Straight debt will not constitute a second class of stock as long as the following conditions are met: (1) interest rate and payment dates cannot be linked to profits, dividends, or borrower discretion; (2) conversion into stock or other equity interests is not possible; and (3) the individual, estate, or trust holding the obligation is eligible to be a shareholder in an S corporation. The 1996 Tax Act expanded this exception to permit straight debt to be held by any person who is regularly and actively engaged in the business of lending money. Note that straight debt may cause an S corporation termination if the obligation is modified or transferred to an individual who is ineligible to be an S corporation shareholder.

Is it ever a good idea to terminate the S corporation election?

As a rule, once an S corporation becomes profitable, it will be better off terminating the S corporation election and becoming a regular (C) corporation, unless the S corporation is distributing all its income to the shareholders as earned. The reason is that a profitable regular (C) corporation takes dollars off the top of the shareholder-employee's personal tax liability; the exact amount of earnings to be left in the corporation is fairly flexible, since the shareholder-employee is ordinarily drawing a tax-deductible salary. Further, there are other means to avoid having a payment characterized as a nondeductible dividend. One well-established approach is to implement a comprehensive fringe benefit program. For example, whereas the rules respecting pension and profit-sharing plans are basically the same for regular (C) and S corporations, there are important differences. Most notably, shareholder-employees of an S corporation may not borrow from their corporate plans without violating the prohibited transaction rules. When it comes to other fringe benefits, such as medical payment plans, the law treats any owner of more than 2 percent of an S corporation like a partner, so C corporation status becomes much more advantageous.

Name some tax-deductible fringe benefits that can be provided tax-free to a shareholder-employee but that need not be provided to substantially all full-time employees on a nondiscriminatory basis.

Free meals and housing on company premises
Free parking
Medical examinations
Payment of professional and business club dues
Subscriptions to business publications
De minimis fringe benefits

Name some tax-deductible fringe benefits that can be provided tax-free to a shareholder-employee but that must also be provided to substantially all full-time employees on a nondiscriminatory basis.

$50,000 of group term life insurance
Tuition reimbursement plans
Pensions and profit-sharing plans
Child and dependent care, subject to limitations
Recreational and health facilities

What is the function of "basis"?

Basis is primarily used in measuring the amount of gain or loss realized on the sale, exchange, or other disposition of property. It is also used for such purposes as determining the amount of depreciation or amortization allowable to an asset. Several methods are used in determining initial basis. In most cases, a taxpayer's initial basis in an asset is equal to the cost of the asset ("cost basis"). Thus, if Jones spends $10,000 for a piece of machinery, his initial basis in the machinery is $10,000. In certain cases, a taxpayer's initial basis is established by reference to somebody else's basis ("carryover basis"). As an example, if property is received by gift, generally the donee will take the donor's basis. In other cases, a taxpayer's basis on one asset may be transferred to another asset owned by the taxpayer ("substituted basis"). As an example of substituted basis, Kelly's basis in her partnership interest includes her basis in the property she contributed to the business. As a further example of carryover basis, the partnership's basis in property contributed to it generally equals the contributing partner's basis in that property. Regardless of the method used to determine initial basis, said amount will be increased or decreased to record subsequent events having a tax effect. Thus, if machinery costing $10,000 is depreciated on a straight-line basis over a 10-year period, then, assuming no salvage value, the annual depreciation deduction is $1,000, and the corporation's adjusted basis after the first year is $9,000.

What is a shareholder's initial basis in a stock?

The initial basis includes cash and the basis of any property contributed to the corporation as well as the amount of any gain recognized when the property was contributed to the corporation. Thus, if you contribute $10,000 to ABC Corporation in consideration for the issuance of 100 shares of common stock, your tax basis in the shares is $10,000. If two years later, the shares are sold for $100,000, your tax basis in the shares is still $10,000, and your gain on the sale is $90,000.

What are the tax consequences of forming a corporation?

Generally, a gain or loss is recognized when an asset is exchanged. However, Section 351 of the Internal Revenue Code is an important exception to this rule and, when the requirements are met, mandates that no gain or loss need be recognized on corporate formation, and that the basis of the transferred property carries over to the transferee corporation, with the transferor having the same basis in the corporate stock or securities as he or she had in the transferred property. Proceeds from the issuance of stock are never taxable income to the corporation because they do not constitute earnings—instead, these proceeds are in the nature of capital contributions. All of this means that the corporation will not receive a step-up to fair market value for the property acquired. Rather, the corporation will receive a basis that is carried over from the transferor. The transferor will not receive a market value basis for the stock obtained—rather, the stock will assume a carryover basis from the property transferred. For example, Bob transfers property with a tax basis of $5,000 to a corporation in exchange for all its shares. Notwithstanding the fair market value of the property or the stock, the corporation's tax basis in the property is $5,000 and Bob's stock basis is $5,000. Any inherent gain or loss will not be recognized until the property or stock is actually sold. For Section 351 to apply, the following requirements must be met: There must be a transfer of property to the corporation (such property includes money, machinery, buildings, land, and similar items and also includes patents, leases, secret processes, and other forms of know-how, but does not include services, past, present, or future); the property must be transferred solely in exchange for stock or securities of the corporation (such stock may be common or preferred, voting or nonvoting, but not stock rights, warrants, options, or convertible bonds; such securities may include long-term debt, that is, with at least five years left to maturity); and the person or group of persons who transferred the property must have control of the corporation immediately after the exchange (the term "person" includes all entities legally treated as such, meaning individuals, corporations, partnerships, trusts, and estates; "control" means ownership of at least 80 percent of the combined voting power of all classes of stock entitled to vote and at least 80 percent of the total number of shares of all other classes of stock; and "immediately after the exchange" means an orderly execution of a previously defined agreement but does not necessarily require a simultaneous exchange.) If the control requirement is not satisfied, any realized gains will be subject to immediate recognition.

What disclosure must be made to the IRS of a Section 351 exchange?

The transferor in a Section 351 exchange attaches a disclosure statement to the tax return for the tax year in which the exchange occurs. The disclosure must contain the following information: (1) a description of the property transferred, including its costs; (2) the fair market value of the stock received, the type of stock, and the number of shares of each class of stock received; and (3) the amount and nature of the liabilities transferred, including the business purpose for the transfer. The corporation, in turn, files a statement with its own return for the year of the exchange. The corporate statement must contain the following information: (1) a description of the property received from the transferor, and its cost basis; (2) the total shares issued and outstanding before and after the exchange, the classes of stock, and the fair market value of each class on the date of exchange; (3) the amount and nature of the liabilities assumed, the business purpose for their transfer, and the circumstances of their creation; (4) the amount of money paid to the transferor; and (5) a description of any other property delivered to the transferor (see the discussion of "boot"), its basis, and its fair market value on the date of the transfer.

What happens if a transferor receives only securities in the exchange?

Each person transferring assets to the corporation must have an equity interest in the new corporation; hence, an exchange in which a transferor only receives securities will not qualify. Further, if appreciated property is exchanged for stock and securities, the transferor must recognize gain to the extent of the securities received. (See the discussion of "boot".)

Does Section 351 work with a postincorporation transfer?

Yes. A postincorporation transfer can be treated as a Section 351 tax-free exchange so long as the transferors receive stock or securities in the corporation and, as a group, they control the corporation immediately after the transfer. Note, though, that if a transfer of assets in exchange for stock or securities does not qualify under Section 351, it will be treated as a sale with the transferor required to recognize any gain or loss on the transfer. Of course, if the transferor doesn't receive anything at all in the exchange, the transaction is simply treated as a contribution to the capital of the corporation and a tax-free increase in the corporation's capital.

Aren't there exceptions to this rule regarding tax-free incorporation?

Yes. There are three major exceptions. The first exception is known as the "boot" exception. The second exception is called the "liabilities in excess of basis" exception. The third exception is called the services exception.

What is the "boot" exception?

A contribution of property to a corporation will be tax-free only if the person contributing property receives stock or long-term debt obligations of the corporation in exchange. If other property is received "to boot," the property transferred will be partly or fully taxable depending on the fair market value of the boot received. For example, if you transfer $10,000 for 100 shares of a newly formed corporation, your basis in the shares will be $10,000 and no gain will be recognized. If you transfer equipment with a fair market value of $10,000 and a tax basis of $1,000 for 100 shares of a newly formed corporation, your tax basis will be $1,000 in the shares and none of the $9,000 gain will be immediately recognized. Rather, the gain will be recognized only when the property or stock is sold. However, if you make the same transfer but receive, say, 50 shares and $5,000 of short-term debt, you have received property other than stock or long-term debt ("boot") in the amount of $5,000, which means that $5,000 of the $9,000 gain must be recognized. Regardless of the amount of boot received in an exchange, you recognize only the lesser of the fair market value of the boot received in the exchange or the realized gain (here, the lesser of $5,000 or $9,000).

What is the character of the income from the boot?

The character of the income the shareholders must report when they receive boot depends on the kind of assets being transferred. Thus, if a sale of an asset would have produced capital gain, the boot income is capital gain, but if a sale of the asset would have produced ordinary income, the boot income is treated as ordinary income.

What happens if there is a realized loss?

A realized loss will not be deductible. It will be deferred. Suppose you transfer property with a tax basis of $1,500 and a fair market value of $1,000 for $700 of stock and $300 in cash. The amount realized is the consideration received, or $1,000. Since the tax basis is $1,500, the loss realized is $500. The boot received here—the cash—is $300 and the deductible loss is zero. This means that although there is a realized loss of $500, none of that loss will be deductible; regardless of whether boot is received in a Section 351 exchange, losses are not recognized.

What is the tax effect of "boot" on basis?

If the transferor receives only stock or securities from the transferee corporation, the basis in the shares is the same as the basis in the transferred property, but if boot is received by the transferor in addition, the basis of the stock or securities will equal the basis of the transferred property plus any gain recognized by the transferor on the exchange minus the cash or the fair market value of the boot received. Meanwhile, the transferee's basis in the property received will be the same as the transferor's basis plus any gain recognized by the transferor as a result of the exchange.

What happens if more than one property is transferred?

In certain cases, more than one property may be transferred in the exchange, as when an operating proprietorship decides to incorporate. The principle here is that the calculations are done on an asset-by-asset basis with any boot received in the exchange allocated in proportion to the fair market value of each asset and not its relative adjusted basis value. Assume that property is transferred with an $800 tax basis and a fair market value of $1,000 in exchange for $600 in stock and $400 in cash. The first asset has a tax basis of $500 and a fair market value of $300, the second asset has a tax basis of $100 and a fair market value of $400, and the third asset has a tax basis of $200 and a fair market value of $300. The first asset reflects a loss of $200, the second asset reflects a gain of $300, and the third asset reflects a gain of $100, for a total realized gain of $200. The total fair market value of $1,000 is allocated among the three assets as follows: 30 percent to the first asset, 40 percent to the second asset, and 30 percent to the third asset. When those percentages are applied to the $400 of boot (i.e., the cash), 30 percent of the $400, or $120, is allocated to the first asset; 40 percent of the $400, or $160, is allocated to the second asset; and 30 percent of the $400, or $120, is allocated to the third asset. The gain recognized for the first asset is $0 (there is a realized loss), the gain recognized for the second asset is $160, and the gain recognized for the third asset is $120. The boot received is thus allocated in proportion to each asset's relative fair market value. The total gain recognized does not include any loss recognition for the first asset.

201

Explain the "liabilities in excess of basis" exception.

Generally, a corporation's assumption of a liability—or its acquisition of an asset subject to a liability—neither disqualifies the transaction from tax-free status nor produces taxable income to the shareholders (i.e., it is *not* considered to be boot). Although the corporation will take a carryover basis in the property, the transferor's basis in the stock is decreased by the amount of the liability assumed. However, if a transfer is motivated by tax avoidance or if the corporation does not have a bona fide business purpose for assuming a liability, the corporation's assumption of a liability, will be treated as boot. For example, if you contribute property encumbered by a $30,000 mortgage to ABC Corporation in exchange for 100 shares of common stock, and your tax basis in the property is $20,000, your taxable income resulting from the contribution will be $10,000. This determination is made on a shareholder-by-shareholder basis with all of the assets and liabilities transferred by each shareholder aggregated to make the finding.

Explain the services exception.

Stock received for services performed for a corporation does not qualify as property and therefore is treated as compensation to the transferor. Moreover, a recipient of stock issued solely for services to be performed, or already performed, does not count for purposes of satisfying the 80 percent test. Note, however, that if both property is transferred and services are performed by the transferor, all the stock that person receives for the assets and services is considered in determining whether the control test has been met.

Are there times when it might be better for an incorporation to be taxable?

Yes. There may be times when it is desirable to avoid the application of Section 351 and for the transfer to be treated as a taxable event (i.e., a taxable sale). In such a case, the transferee-corporation will take a higher basis in the property—a basis equal to the fair market value of the property. The transferor will recognize gain and therefore ordinarily have a lower taxable gain on the later disposition of the stock. Examples of situations warranting such treatment include the following: The transferor has unused net operating losses and can use the carryover to offset the gain from the incorporation; an asset with a built-in loss is transferred to the corporation (although Section 351 doesn't permit loss recognition, making the exchange a taxable event will generally permit the transferor to recognize the loss immediately); and a corporation makes a Section 338 election when it acquires a subsidiary (with the passage of the Tax Reform Act of 1986, a Section 338 election is ordinarily inadvisable other than with respect to the acquisition of a subsidiary from a consolidated group as set forth in Section 338(h)(10)). Note: There are various ways to disqualify an exchange and make a transfer taxable, such as by deliberately failing the control test.

What is the tax effect of a corporation suffering losses?

It is common for a start-up enterprise to incur losses in the early years. If a regular (C) corporation is used, such losses will result in no tax benefit to the individual shareholders, since the losses belong to the corporation. Had the S corporation election been in effect, however, such losses would pass through to the respective shareholders and be deductible by them against their other income. Further, if stock qualifies as Section 1244 stock and becomes worthless, the stock is treated as an ordinary loss to the extent of $50,000 for a single taxpayer and $100,000 for a married taxpayer filing a joint return. This is the case whether the corporation was a regular (C) corporation or an S corporation. (Note: Section 1244 stock is common or preferred stock issued in exchange for cash or property other than stock or securities of the issuer or another company; at the time of issuance, the aggregate amount of money and property that the corporation has received must not exceed $1 million.)

For individuals, capital losses may be offset only against capital gains plus $3,000 per year. Does Section 1244 allow the shareholder to deduct a loss without this limitation?

Yes. Qualifying losses under Section 1244 are subject to a maximum deduction of $100,000 for married couples or $50,000 for single taxpayers. Any excess loss is then subject to the capital loss limitation, however. The Section 1244 ordinary loss is considered to be a business loss for purposes of computing a net operating loss (NOL). In a carryover year with multiple operating losses, however, the $50,000 and $100,000 thresholds will not limit the NOL deduction. Note that when the basis of the contributed property exceeds the market value, the property will have a built-in capital loss and the allowable loss under Section 1244 is limited. Assume, for example, that a taxpayer receives Section 1244 stock contributing property to the business with a basis of $5,000 and a fair market value of $1,000. The taxpayer will thus acquire a basis in the stock of $5,000. Under Section 1244, the taxpayer's basis in the stock is $1,000 (reduced by the $4,000 built-in capital loss). If the taxpayer sells the stock for $500, the built-in capital loss will still be $4,000, and the $500 loss will be an ordinary loss.

What taxpayers may benefit from Section 1244?

The benefits of Section 1244 are allowed only to individual taxpayers. Trusts and estates are specifically excluded, as are corporations. An individual partner in a partnership may qualify if the taxpayer was a partner when the stock was originally issued to the partnership. The stock must be held continuously by the partnership after issuance.

The partner deducts his or her pro rata share of the loss sustained. Under the original investor rule, only an original investor in qualifying stock can take an ordinary loss deduction. Thus, under Section 1244, if the stock is not acquired directly from the issuing corporation, that stock will not qualify. This means that stock acquired from another party by gift or purchase will not qualify. Further, stock will not qualify under Section 1244 for any subsequent buyer if the stock is first issued to an investment firm and later resold. The qualifying stock must be continuously held by the individual or partnership that sustains the loss. If a partnership distributes stock to a partner, the partner will not qualify as an original investor.

What is a qualifying small business corporation?

As noted, preferred and common stock can qualify for Section 1244 treatment, and the corporation should maintain stock records indicating who received the stock, when the stock was issued, and the amount and type of consideration received. For the stock to come from a qualifying small business corporation, the capital contribution (including paid-in capital surplus) may not exceed $1 million at the time of issuance of the stock. This $1 million includes both money and other property received by the corporation for its stock. When property is contributed to the corporation, the value included in the $1 million test is the adjusted basis of the corporation less any liabilities assumed by the corporation. Further, the corporation must meet a source income test. Under this test, the corporation must derive its income from a trade or business—that is, more than half of the corporation's gross receipts for the five preceding years must be from sources other than royalties, rents, dividends, interest, annuities, and gains from the sale of stock. For corporations not in existence for five years, the source income test applies to all preceding years. Note that Section 1244 stock must be issued in exchange for money or other property but not for other stock or securities. Stock issued in exchange for services rendered to the issuing corporation is disqualified. The reason is that stock issued for services is not considered to be a capital investment. If stock is issued in exchange for the cancellation of corporate debt owed to the taxpayer, the cancellation of indebtedness qualifies as an exchange for money or other property under Section 1244. However, a cancellation of indebtedness is disqualified if the debt was created by the performance of personal services or is evidenced by security. Note that only the initial capital investment for a direct stock issuance will qualify under Section 1244. Additional stock for a subsequent contribution may qualify, but if the taxpayer contributes additional capital and the corporation does not issue new stock, the investment will not qualify for Section 1244 treatment.

What happens to a shareholder's basis in Section 1244 stock if additional contributions are made?

A shareholder's basis in Section 1244 stock is not adjusted for additional capital contributions. Rather, the basis of the stock contributed will become the basis of the newly issued Section 1244 stock. Assume that a shareholder was issued 100 shares of Section 1244 stock in exchange for $1,000 in 1999. Then, in 2000, the shareholder contributed $500 capital to the corporation, increasing the tax basis in the shares to $1,500. Also in 2000, the shareholder sells all 100 shares for $800, resulting in a loss of $700. Two thirds of the loss ($1000/$1500) thus is allocated to the Section 1244 stock. The balance of the loss does not qualify for Section 1244 treatment.

How does a shareholder prove that Section 1244 stock has become worthless?

To claim a loss on Section 1244 stock that is not sold or exchanged, the shareholder must have evidence that the stock has no realizable value (i.e., is worthless). All the information available to prove worthlessness should be marshaled at the time of the loss and retained in case of audit.

How are earnings and profits (E&P) calculated?

The tax law does not define earnings and profits specifically, but does require a number of adjustments to reach E&P. Essentially, the company's taxable income is adjusted for specific deductions and increases. The purpose of making these adjustments is to convert taxable income so it more correctly reflects the entity's gains and losses. Thus, depreciation for E&P is computed on a straight-line basis and accelerated depreciation is not allowed. In any case, deductions from taxable income required to reach E&P include the following: nondeductible expenses, federal income taxes paid or accrued, shareholder distributions, and excess charitable contributions. Increases to taxable income required to compute E&P include the following: tax-exempt income, dividends-received deductions, NOL carryovers and carrybacks, LIFO inventory recapture, and capital loss carryovers deducted in the current year.

If a regular (C) corporation has earnings and profits, how is a corporate distribution to the shareholders taxed?

If a regular (C) corporation has earnings and profits (E&P), a distribution of cash or property will be fully taxable to the recipient as a dividend. Once E&P has been reduced to zero however, such distributions will be tax-free until the shareholder receives an amount equal to his or her basis in the shares, and thus the basis has been reduced to zero. Thereafter, any distributions will be taxed as capital gain. For example, assume that you own 200 shares of the ABC Corporation with a tax basis of $10,000, and the corporation has E&P of $10,000. For the current tax year, the corporation makes a distribution of $25,000. The distribution is taxable to you as follows: the first $10,000 is taxable as a dividend, the next $10,000 reduces your basis in your shares down to $0, and the next $5,000 is taxable to you as a capital gain. Even if the corporation records a loss for the current year, so long as accumulated E&P exceeds the distribution, a dividend will result. (Note: The rules are somewhat different for an S corporation with E&P.)

What is the tax effect to the corporation of a distribution?

In the case of a cash distribution, generally, the corporation recognizes no gain or loss unless the transfer is of a liquidating distribution. The reason is that dividends represent distributions of the corporation's after-tax profits, so that the corporation's earnings and profits are reduced by the amount of the cash distribution. If appreciated property is distributed to shareholders, however, the corporation must recognize taxable gain to the extent that the property's fair market value exceeds its adjusted basis. The distribution is treated as though the property were sold at its fair market value to the shareholder and if the property transfer is subject to a liability, the fair market value of the property cannot be less than the liability.

Overall, how can the tax treatment of distributions by a regular (C) corporation be characterized?

A corporate distribution is a payment made to a shareholder that may or may not be taxable to the recipient. If the business operates at a profit, a distribution from the corporation's earnings will be a taxable dividend; if the corporation does not have accumulated earnings and profits, a distribution is considered to be a tax-free recovery of capital investment. In the case of *cash* distributions, such disbursements constitute a taxable dividend to the extent of current earnings and profits, a taxable dividend to the extent of accumulated earnings and profits from prior years, a nontaxable return of capital to the extent of basis if there are no earnings and profits, and a taxable gain from the sale of stock if there are no earnings and profits or stock basis. Should the distribution exceed the earnings and profits and the stockholder's stock basis, the sale is ordinarily a capital gain. However, the gain qualifies as capital only if the stock is a capital asset in the shareholder's hands. The corporation will recognize no gain or loss for such a cash distribution unless the transfer is for a liquidating distribution. The corporation's earnings and profits are thus reduced by the amount of the cash distributions. Although dividends may reduce earnings and profits, they are not considered operating expenses, and are thus nondeductible disbursements. In the case of property distributions, the fair market value of the property may not equal its tax basis, so there will be a gain or loss inherent in the transfer. Thus, if appreciated property is distributed to a shareholder, any taxable gain is realized by the corporation and not by the shareholder. Again, if a corporation distributes property to the shareholders, the amount received is determined by that property's fair market value, with the amount of the distribution reduced by any liabilities assumed by the shareholder or any liabilities to which the transferred property is subject. For this purpose, the shareholder receives a basis in the property acquired equal to its fair market value on the date of distribution. After the property's fair market value is established, the taxability to the stockholder is determined in the same manner as for cash distributions: (1) taxable dividend to the extent of earnings and profits, (2) nontaxable distribution to the extent of stock basis, and (3) taxable gain on sale if earnings and profits and stock basis are exhausted. From the corporation's standpoint, if appreciated property is distributed, the corporation recognizes taxable gain measured by the excess of the property's fair market value over its basis. Thus, the distribution is treated as though the property were sold at its fair market value to the shareholder so that if the property transferred is subject to a liability, the fair market value of the property cannot be less than the liability. Assume, therefore, that a company distributes appreciated property to a shareholder and that the property's fair market value is $100,000 and its tax basis is $50,000. The property transferred is subject to a mortgage of $80,000. The taxable gain to the corporation is $30,000 ($80,000 − $50,000). From the shareholder's standpoint, the amount of the distribution is reduced by the liability. Thus, the amount distributed to the shareholder is $20,000 ($100,000 − $80,000).

I want to form an S corporation. I understand that preferred stock is not permitted in the capital structure of an S corporation, but what about debt?

Debt could be an alternative. As mentioned previously, distributions to shareholders are nondeductible; however, loans made by the shareholders generally result in tax-deductible interest. With that in mind, many corporations are motivated to an excessive level of debt versus equity and risk IRS recharacterization of the debt as equity and the interest payments as dividends. The IRS looks at a number of factors to determine if an obligation is really debt. First, there should be a note, which is an unqualified promise to pay principal and interest. The obligation should be treated as such not just on the tax returns but in all of the corporate financial and other records. The debt should have a fixed maturity date. If the debt is to be paid in installments, a definite repayment plan should exist and be followed. The corporation must be required to pay a reasonable rate of interest and the rate (and payments) should not hinge on corporate earnings. Second, the shareholder-creditor should be able to enforce the debt, the debt should not be convertible into stock, and the shareholder debt should not be subordinated to that of a bank or other commercial lender. Although a bank or other lender would understandably wish to subordinate such a debt, such a practice is inherently suspect to the IRS. Relatedly, debt issued proportionately to share ownership in a company is more likely to look like equity. Thus, if two shareholders each own 50 percent of the capital and 50 percent of the debt, this proportionality of interest leads to a finding of equity. Further, the IRS will look to the debt-equity ratio. For this purpose, both inside debt and outside debt will be included in the debt figure, so that a thinly capitalized business (i.e., one with a high debt-equity ratio) is more likely to have its so-called debt recharacterized as additional equity. In sum, a good test to remember is whether an independent creditor would have made the loan to the corporation under similar circumstances. If so, recharacterization of the debt as equity is less likely.

Explain the limitation on basis applicable to S corporations.

The pass-through of S corporations, like that of partnerships, is limited by basis, but the liabilities of an S corporation are not included in the shareholders' basis, thereby limiting the amount of losses that can flow through to the shareholders and making distribution of any refinancing proceeds taxable to shareholders.

What is the built-in gains tax?

If a former C corporation elects S status, the built-in gains tax may apply. This tax imposes a corporate-level tax on the net recognized built-in gain during the recognition period. The recognition period is the 10-year period beginning with the first day of the first taxable year for which the corporation was an S corporation. This period is extended to include any property sold in an installment sale during such period. Thus, the net recognized built-in gain is an annual limit on the amount of built-in gain subject to tax. The amount of tax is limited to the lesser of: (1) the amount of the taxable income of the S corporation for the taxable year, taking into account only the recognized built-in gains, recognized built-in losses, and recognized built-in carryovers; (2) the taxable income of the S corporation for the year determined as if it were a C corporation, with some modifications; and (3) the amount by which the net unrealized built-in gain exceeds the net recognized built-in gains for all prior taxable years.

For example, assume that Boulder Corporation elects S status for the calendar year 2000. As of January 1, 2000, Boulder holds only real estate with a tax basis of $50,000 and a fair market value of $100,000. On May 1, 2000, Boulder is liquidated, at which time the value of the real estate rises to $200,000. The recognized built-in gain is $150,000 unless Boulder can prove that the real estate's value on January 1, 2000 was $100,000, in which case the recognized built-in gain would be $50,000 (i.e., the gain would be reduced by the post S election appreciation).

What is the effect of having a recognized built-in gain?

If an S corporation has a net recognized built-in gain during the recognition period, the tax is payable at the maximum corporate rate (i.e., 35 percent). Whereas an S corporation is not generally allowed to use any carryovers from the period in which it was a C corporation, the S corporation will be allowed to offset any recognized built-in gains with a net operating loss carryover or capital loss carryover from a C corporation year.

What else can happen if a corporation elects S status?

If the S corporation has C corporation earnings and profits (E&P) and more than 25 percent of its income is passive investment income, then the S corporation is subject to tax at the highest corporate rate (currently 35 percent). Thus, the tax on excess net passive income is levied at the rate of 35 percent with the pass-through of the net passive income to the S corporation shareholders then reduced by the amount of tax imposed. This reduction for the applicable tax is then passed through in the same year as the net passive income, although the tax is typically paid after the year end. Next, if an S corporation that has accumulated E&P from a prior C year makes a distribution to its shareholders, then the portion of the distribution that does not exceed the accumulated adjustments account (which is basically undistributed S corporation profits) is generally nontaxable; the portion of the distribution then is treated as a taxable dividend to the extent that it does not exceed the amount of the accumulated E&P of the former C corporation; finally, the remainder is treated as a return of basis and then as a gain from the sale or exchange of property. Although the election of S status is considered as a mere change in form and does not require investment credit recapture, there are special implications for corporations using the LIFO (last in, first out) method in that a LIFO method C corporation electing to become an S corporation must recapture the benefit of the LIFO method in the year it so elects. Finally, no carryforward or carryback arising for a taxable year in which a corporation is a C corporation may be carried to a taxable year in which it is an S corporation. In sum, when the built-in gains tax applies, the combined S corporation and shareholder-level tax will be huge because the S corporation is subject to a 35 percent built-in gains rate and the shareholders, if taxed at the 39.6 percent rate, are subject to a 26 percent rate on ordinary gain and short-term capital gain. The shareholders are also subject to a tax on the pass-through long-term capital gain. This is just at the federal level; any state taxes would lead to even higher effective tax rates.

How does the S corporation compare with the limited liability company?

If the S corporation requirements cannot be met, the limited liability company may be a good option. It combines the S corporation advantage of limited liability and the partnership advantage of flexibility. It offers limited liability to all its members even if they participate in the business. All states have now passed legislation allowing the limited liability company to be established. Generally, this entity is formed by filing articles of organization with the secretary of state's office, and it may conduct any lawful business activities except those that are expressly prohibited to it (insurance, banking, etc.) Most state laws allow the members to decide how to manage the business. Generally, there is an operating agreement to govern the management of the business. It is similar to a limited partnership agreement under which the members can generally reserve all management powers for themselves or delegate such powers to one or more appointed managers. Neither the members nor the managers will be liable for the company's debts or liabilities. In the event that the limited liability company is not properly created pursuant to state law, the business conducted may subject the members or managers to liability to third parties. Otherwise, as is the case with limited partnerships, the liability of company members will be limited to unpaid capital contributions. The right to transfer a limited liability interest is generally governed by the operating agreement. However, subject to state law, unless a proposed transfer is unanimously approved by the remaining members, the transferee cannot generally participate in the company's management or become a member. This means that the transferee would be allowed to receive only that share of profits and return of capital to which the assigning member would otherwise be entitled. Note that a limited liability company is dissolved upon the occurrence of any of the following events: (1) the expiration of the period fixed in the articles of incorporation; (2) the unanimous written agreement of the parties; (3) the death, retirement, resignation, expulsion, bankruptcy, or dissolution of a member; or (4) any other event that terminates the participation of a member in the limited liability company. A limited liability company is taxed at the federal level as a partnership. Since the S corporation limits the number of shareholders to 75, the limited liability company may be a good alternative. These restrictions are important because they are applicable not only at formation but for the continued operation of the business. Note that a limited liability company has more flexibility than an S corporation in the allocation of specific items of income and expense. A member's share of the limited liability company's income, gain, loss, deduction, or credit is generally allocated under the company's operating agreement as long as it meets the partnership tax regulations dealing with substantial economic effect. Note that where appreciated or depreciated property is contributed to the business, the use of an S corporation may present an opportunity to shift precontribution gain or loss. Such opportunity is not available under the partnership tax rules. Also, whereas an S corporation shareholder can deduct losses up to his or her basis in stock and loans to the corporation, a partner's basis in a partnership interest is increased by his or her allocable share of partnership debt. This permits limited liability members to deduct losses in excess of their cash investment in the company and to receive distributions in excess of the cash invested and previously allocated income without recognizing additional taxable income or gain. Thus, if four investors each contribute $10,000 to a newly formed S corporation and the S corporation borrows $100,000, each investor receives an initial tax basis in the stock of $10,000, even if the investor personally guarantees the corporation's debt. However, if the investors decide to contribute $10,000 each to form a general partnership, and the partnership borrows $100,000, each investor—as an equal partner—receives an initial basis in the partnership interest of $35,000. Since a limited liability company is taxed as a partnership, it is important to note that distributions of appreciated property by an S corporation result in income recognition at the corporate level, while a partnership can generally distribute property to its partners without any partnership-level income recognition. Further, upon the transfer of an ownership interest, the partnership rules allow the purchasing partner to step up his share of the basis in partnership assets if the partnership makes a proper election. Note further that although a partnership can be created by an oral agreement, limited liability status must be formally adopted. Special rules apply at the state level—thus, in the state of Texas, a limited liability company is subject to state franchise tax. A limited liability company offers much of the same flexibility as a partnership; in addition, unlike limited liability partners, owners of a limited liability company are generally free to be active in the management of the business.

How are limited liability companies qualified for federal tax purposes?

Since limited liability companies are treated for federal tax purposes like partnerships, it is useful to review some partnership tax principles. Generally, no gain or loss is recognized on a contribution of money or property to a partnership. The partnership in turn recognizes no gain or loss on the receipt of contributed property from a partner. Thus, a key reason for operating a business in this form is that property may be contributed or distributed on a tax-free basis, without recognition of gain or loss by either the partnership or the partner. Once a contribution to the partnership qualifies for nonrecognition treatment, the firm's tax basis in the contributed property is the same as the property's basis for the contributing partner. Thus, ordinarily the firm takes a carryover basis in the property. Should the exchange be partially taxable, however, the basis of the contributed property is increased by any gain recognized by the partner. To the extent that gain is recognized on the exchange, and the property's basis in the firm's hands exceeds the basis in the transferor's hands, the partnership is treated as if it had placed the property's increased basis portion in service on the contribution date. The partnership's holding period for the property received in the exchange includes the holding period of the transferor. There are a number of exceptions to nonrecognition treatment (i.e., where gain is recognized). Some of the principal exceptions are as follows: (1) where there has been a contribution of services to a partnership in exchange for a partnership interest; (2) where the contribution has been made to an investment company; and (3) where the transaction is actually a sale. If the contribution is followed shortly by a distribution to the contributing partner, the transaction may be recharacterized as a sale or exchange of the property. With that background in mind, it should be noted that although, for federal tax purposes, a limited liability company may actually be taxed as a partnership, a corporation, or an entity separate from its owner (a proprietorship), such companies generally want partnership tax treatment so that members can allocate income and loss in any manner that has substantial economic effect, can include a portion of the company's debt in the tax basis of their interest, and can avoid double taxation on business income. Prior to 1997, an organization's classification for federal tax purposes hinged on the presence of four corporate characteristics: continuity of life, centralization of management, limited liability, and free transferability of interests. An entity was not classified as a corporation unless it possessed more corporate than noncorporate characteristics. Effective January 1, 1997, however, the IRS eliminated this four-factor classification system and adopted a simple check-the-box method that limited liability companies (and other entities) can use to establish their tax classification. The regulations specify certain entities that must be classified as corporations (e.g., insurers) but enable other business entities (called eligible entities) to choose their own classification. Thus, a limited liability company that meets the definition of an eligible entity can receive partnership status for federal tax purposes without having to restructure itself as a partnership. Note that the check-the-box rules apply not just to new entities but to existing entities that are so eligible and desire to change their tax classification. Thus, an existing corporation may wish to change to partnership tax status. Also note that separate rules apply for single-member entities in that the owner of a single-member entity can choose to be recognized as a separate entity classified as a corporation or alternatively disregard the existence of the separate entity. Should the owner disregard the separate existence the business is treated as the same entity as the owner. Should the owner choose to treat the limited liability company as a disregarded entity, separate rules apply for federal employment tax purposes. Ordinarily an employer is responsible for satisfying employment tax obligations; however, if a limited liability company is a disregarded entity, the owner is treated as the employer of the limited liability company's employees, so that the *owner* is responsible for satisfying all employment tax obligations related to those employees.

GLOSSARY

Agency Legal relationship in which one person, the agent, acts on behalf of another person or entity, the principal.

Boot Payment given in addition, "to boot," in an exchange.

Close Corporation Corporation owned by a single individual, or a close-knit group of family or business associates, authorized to conduct business without observing many of the corporate formalities, such as holding annual meetings. Regulations vary by state.

Double Taxation Effect of federal and some state tax legislation, which taxes the same income twice, once as corporate earnings, and again as personal income when dividends are paid.

Estoppel Legal bar that precludes a person from denying that which had been previously affirmed.

Fiscal Year Any 12-month, 52-week, or 365-day period in the financial operations of a governmental or business entity.

Minutes Official written record of the proceedings of a meeting.

Par Value Assigned value of a share of stock, often $1; the price does not necessarily relate to the stock's market value.

RMBCA Revised Model Business Corporation Act.

Sole Proprietorship Unincorporated business owned by one person, who has unlimited liability for the debts of the firm.

Treasury Stock Stock issued publicly by a corporation and reacquired by it, but not canceled.

INDEX